Critical Praise for *BE DiFFERENT or be dead*

Osing demonstrates clearly throughout his book how to create a unique value and service proposition that positions your company differently and vastly ahead of the competition. He has re-energized me to focus on a strategy that truly makes my company indispensable to our customers.

Frank Palmer, CEO
DDB Canada

Keep up the good work... I love it. I keep your book on my car seat beside me... You are my passenger every day in business.

Jason 'Nitroman', CEO NITROLUBE

Roy Osing's *BE DiFFERENT or be dead* is a field guide for those who seek to excel in business. He delivers wisdom and years of experience in bite-sized lessons for success. This book is not simply re-packaging what others have said before, it is different. These are real-life lessons from the coal face, where businesses interface with customers. A must-read.

Darcy Rezac, Managing Director and Chief Engagement Officer
Vancouver Board of Trade and Author, *Work the Pond!*

As someone who has been a part of the chamber of commerce movement for many years, I know many of our member businesses will designate *BE DiFFERENT or be dead* as required reading. In today's uncertain economic environment, entrepreneurs will take comfort from this easy-to-read and informative book.

John Winter, President and CEO
BC Chamber of Commerce

BE DiFFERENT or be dead is an essential read for anyone seeking to achieve real results in their organization.

Don Calder, former President and CEO, BC Telecom
former CEO, Vancouver Whistler 2010 Bid Corporation

Based on over thirty years' experience in marketing and the business community, Roy Osing provides a very clear and concise guide on how to stand out from the crowd in any competitive marketplace. This simple and straightforward book is a must-have for anyone trying to differentiate themselves and succeed in today's economy.

John Gustavson, President and Chief Executive Officer
Canadian Marketing Association

Business is all about relationships/partnerships, understanding our customers' business and their needs, and creating solutions to grow their business. *BE DiFFERENT or be dead* is a definite aid for better 'service, service, service' thinking for our customers. It will teach you how best to brand your business and brand yourself.

Jim 'JJ' Johnston, General Manager
Corus Radio Vancouver

As a former CEO of a national telecommunications company, I can attest to the critical importance for corporate and product differentiation. Osing's passion for business and belief in the need for companies to differentiate themselves from the pack is not just theory: it is based on practical experience that everyone involved in product strategy and management needs.

Carol Stephenson, Dean of Richard Ivey School of Business
The University of Western Ontario

Every business must have a vision of how it is going to be effective in the marketplace. This book is one of the most useful I have seen in making sure that you choose the right vision. It is a must-read for anyone interested in superior business leadership.

Bill McCourt, professional mentor to CEOs, former CEO

Roy Osing's new book provides great in-depth reference material for business consultants assisting owners in designing, implementing and monitoring a successful business strategy.

Colin Brown, Business Consultant
ROCG Americas LLC

BE DiFFERENT is the first business book I've read in twenty years that I didn't find boring. It's not a textbook. It's a hands-on, how-to manual and should become a well-used reference guide for business people everywhere. I commend Roy Osing for this fine addition to business education.

Mark Cullen, Corporate Director

For thirty years I have been working with leadership teams — in both large organizations and small start-ups — to take the performance of their organization to a new level. Roy Osing offers a rich and stimulating source of practical action for delighting customers and separating your organization from the pack — a must-read for anyone interested in what really works.

Lorne Armstrong, President
Armstrong Consulting Group

A remarkably concise yet extensive course in some of the best management practices for today's turbulent business world. Great tips that can be put to use instantly!

Don Babick, Corporate Director
former President and COO, Canwest Publications

As a business leader for many different businesses over the years, I have learned the value of not just having a good strategy but, more importantly, the tireless execution of that strategy. Never have I found a business book that ties these two concepts together so well while offering so many practical and effective ways for an organization to enhance its performance.

Tom Brauser, Vice President — Operations
Intrawest ULC

Not just another management book, BE DiFFERENT or be dead is a how-to manual for executives. Read it, read it again, draft your road-map and prepare to reap the benefits of a Be Different organization.

Mike Watson, President
Ignite Management Services Ltd.

Roy articulates how companies can compete and win using more unique attributes rather than best price. I found it personally very useful and timely to review his 'how to' on sustainable differentiation, so I could simplify and better communicate our own strategy.

Chris Catliff, President and CEO
North Shore Credit Union

True to its title, this book is remarkably different than the myriad of business books those of us committed to leadership have read. Knowing Roy Osing from his work, we benefited greatly from many of his principles and approaches — these concepts will help you love and dazzle your customers!

Arthur R. Tymos, President and Chief Executive Officer
Creation Technologies

Who would have predicted the demise of so many venerable firms that we have witnessed in the past year? Those who dare to be different will survive; the rest will slowly fade away. *BE DiFFERENT or be dead* will help you align every part of your organization to be unique, different and consequently survive and indeed thrive!

Terry Taciuk, President
Vancity Insurance

In *BE DiFFERENT or be dead*, Roy Osing has condensed the wisdom and street-smarts gleaned from a stellar career as a senior executive into a practical and accessible guide for today's — and tomorrow's — leaders. I heartily recommend *BE DiFFERENT or be dead* for anyone who cares about customers, competition and career success.

Rick Knowlan, President
Knowlan Consulting Group Inc.

Osing cuts through the inspirational jargon with which many business texts distract their readers and provides a practical and concrete framework that can be customized to suit both large and small enterprises. *BE DiFFERENT* does exactly what it recommends its readers to do: cuts the crap and focuses on execution.

Trek
The Magazine of The University of British Columbia, Vancouver

BE DiFFERENT or be dead

47 143403

www.bedifferentorbedead.com

BE DiFFERENT or be dead
Your Business Survival Guide

Roy Osing

GRANVILLE ISLAND
PUBLISHING

Library and Archives Canada Cataloguing in Publication

Osing, Roy, 1946-
Be different or be dead: your business survival guide / Roy Osing.
— 2nd ed.
Includes index.

ISBN 978-1-894694-69-8

1. Industrial management.

2. Success in business. I. Title.

HD62.7.O835 2009   658   C2009-900083-0

Editor: Gordon Thomas
Proofreader: Renate Preuss
Indexer: bookmark: editing & indexing
Cover design: Andrew Johnstone
Jacket design: Omar Gallegos
Text design: Omar Gallegos
Author photos: Dee Lippingwell

Granville Island Publishing Ltd.
212–1656 Duranleau St · Granville Island
Vancouver BC · Canada · V6H 3S4
info@granvilleislandpublishing.com
www.granvilleislandpublishing.com

For more information on seminars, workshops and keynote speaking please visit www.bedifferentorbedead.com

First Published April 2009 · Printed in China
Second Edition 2010

Dedication

To my best friend and wife Leilani, whose unconditional support throughout my career as well as her wisdom, playfulness and love enriches and completes my life in so many ways.

Acknowledgements

Among the many people who offered help and support to me during the writing of this book, I wish to express my thanks:

To my wife Leilani, who encouraged me to share my career learnings with others, who offered insightful and stimulating ideas on the book's structure and content, and who tolerated my many early morning sessions on my laptop building my manuscript.

To my Mom, whose strength, drive and passion shaped my life.

To my Dad, for your calm and steady influence that guided me.

To my sons, Colin and Ryan; their wives, Pilar and Michelle; and my precious grandchildren, Reesa, Kohen, Carter and Capri, who have all given me more love, support and encouragement than anyone could possibly expect.

To my closest friends John and Colin and other family members, who were terrific listeners and witnessed the process of writing my book. Thank you for being there with your valuable perspective and unwavering confidence.

To my 'raw' manuscript readers, Lorne & Roxy Armstrong, Brian Canfield, Rick Knowlan, Bill McCourt and Darcy Rezac, for plugging through my initial version and providing me with comments and suggestions for improving my work.

To my publisher, Jo Blackmore, who guided me patiently through the process of getting my work into final form.

To my book designer, Omar Gallegos, who created a brilliant 'look and feel' to the book.

To my editor, Gordon Thomas, who provided invaluable editorial assistance and who gave me confidence that my work would be relevant and meaningful to a wide range of organizations.

And finally, to BC Telecom, its successor TELUS and the many individuals who supported my career and helped shaped my life: Brian Canfield, Darren Entwistle, Terry Heenan, Gordon MacFarlane, Bill McCourt, Judy Shuttleworth, Paul Smith, Leo Dooling, John Rayer and E.R. 'Woody' Lutke, to name but a few. These people were responsible for my very gratifying and rewarding career. Thanks for the many opportunities they provided me to not only learn BE DiFFERENT approaches to business but also to have the freedom to apply them with their full support. While large organizations are rich with learning potential, they don't always make it so abundantly available to its employees. I was fortunate indeed!

Contents

SECTION FIVE

BE DiFFERENT Sales

Foreword

Over the span of my career — indeed, the career of any business-person — certain individuals stand out as memorable and distinctive. Some remain lifetime colleagues and friends long after the formal working relationship ends.

Roy Osing is one such individual.

During my long tenure with BC Telecom and later TELUS, I had the opportunity to work with Roy in a variety of capacities. He possessed an uncanny ability to react to complex situations and challenges quickly, effectively and with a unique personal style that, while often disarmingly frank and direct, was rarely wrong.

Roy speaks on the impacts of exogenous factors. The tele-communications industry is a classic example of having to deal with issues beyond your control. The industry has moved from being suppliers of basic voice and data services to being suppliers of very complex integrated services in an extremely competitive environ-ment, all in a relatively short time frame.

The external enabling factors for this phenomenon are advances in technology and subsequent changes in regulation. Since technology advances move light years faster than regulators can manage change, we enter into an even more challenging environment, which sees an open competitive marketplace still being regulated for the incumbent players. This is a process that I have called 'Regulated Competition'.

The challenge has been to develop a strategy that is focused on customers' emerging needs and organized accordingly. It involves changing the internal cultural thinking to develop the necessary flexibility within the organization to remain financially viable, developing the skills within the employee base to complement the strategy, focusing on where the technology is taking us and what opportunities will be enabled by technology, and finally, focusing on the customer's needs to enable them to be competitive in their fields

All of these issues are factors that Roy has dealt with in his varied roles within our Industry.

I began my career as an apprentice and ended my tenure with BC Telecom as chairman and CEO of the company. I retired in 1997 and remained on as the chair of the board of directors. BC Telecom merged in 1999 with the Alberta-based company TELUS, and I remained as chair. Eight months later I became the CEO of the merged company while the board searched for the CEO who arrived nine months later and is still there today. Upon Darren Entwistle's arrival I returned to the role of the chair of the board, a position in which I still serve.

As a longstanding business professional and executive (I have been with BC Telecom and TELUS since 1956, the sign of a misspent youth!), I clearly understand the challenges facing the global marketplace today. The economic realities we face impact businesses directly and significantly.

The speed of change that we find today in the number of new competitors, the shifting (albeit slowly) regulations to reflect an open market condition, and the general issues with the financial markets requires all the strategic focus that can be brought to the challenge.

The title of this book reflects Roy's direct style and accurate take on this current reality. To ensure an ongoing presence in the marketplace, a business must be distinctive, it must be different, or it faces potential decline and eventual failure. In other words, it will be dead.

Some years ago I and others identified the regulatory changes that would occur and dramatically alter the face of telecommunications in Canada and pose significant economic challenges to the incumbent telephone companies. I also predicted that there would be a consolidation of the players in the industry in order to achieve the scale and scope necessary to successfully compete and grow.

We were not wrong. Times changed, and we had to change with them.

As president of TELUS Advanced Communications, Roy was instrumental as a change agent. He forged multiple strategic partnerships and alliances with major corporations and was responsible for exponential growth in emerging data and Internet businesses, successfully positioning the company as a global leader in 21st century telecommunications.

In *BE DiFFERENT or be dead,* Roy wisely recognizes the need to keep pace with the dynamics impacting a business, and that failure to do so will ultimately be the demise of both small and large enterprises alike.

I wholeheartedly agree with him. Any smart businessperson should as well.

What Roy identifies as his value proposition is simple: ideas that have been successfully implemented and are not based solely on theoretical constructs and principles. In his words, ideas that work.

Anyone who has known Roy or attended his workshops and seminars understands why. His charismatic, no-nonsense approach is engaging and captivating, his knowledge deep and clearly presented. Qualities I recognize in effective leaders, qualities that set them apart.

The business book market is awash in 'how to' manuals on a myriad of topics. Some are better than others, most simply a recapitulation of material that is all too familiar. Most make grandiose promises but few deliver.

Few are truly different.

This book is.

Brian Canfield

Director and Chairman of the Board

TELUS Communications

Introduction

BE DiFFERENT or be dead presents practical and proven ideas that will not only enhance the performance of your organization but also ensure the successful navigation of your business through the turbulent waters of the contemporary marketplace.

My *BE DiFFERENT* guide is based on ideas that I have successfully implemented in my business career over the past thirty-five years. My book is different from standard 'how to' business books. More than simply offering theoretical solutions, it is founded on practical value coupled with sound business principles. If I did not derive successful results from an idea for improving performance that idea didn't make this book.

I will give you ideas based on solid business principles that have been successfully implemented in the real world.

I am sure that at some point you've discovered a great idea with substantial theoretical appeal but were unable to deliver its promised benefits because you couldn't implement it. You're not alone. Many ideas presented in business books are rooted in sound management or leadership principles but provide little direction in terms of how to put them to practical use. This is due in part to the inexperience of many authors who have limited hands-on experience and have not been held accountable for improving results.

Assuming that an idea will somehow get implemented on its theoretical virtue alone is a disaster waiting to happen. We've all witnessed great ideas go down in flames because they couldn't get past the great idea stage.

In contrast, I'm offering you ideas that are grounded in sound business principles and have been successfully implemented in the real world. They have harnessed the emotional energy of people in a variety of organizations who are willing to step forward and try something different.

I believe in providing step-by-step directions on how to deliver the various ideas I offer to you. Simply stated, the following illustrates the difference between my approach and more conventional approaches:

Conventional Approach ⟶ Good ideas founded in accepted business doctrine.

Be Different Approach ⟶ Innovative ideas founded in solid business principles with a proven track record of successful implementation, demonstrated results and turned-on people who are excited by them!

I was fortunate to work in rich environments that enabled me to develop new ideas. I was a career learner and spent copious amounts of time and energy in whatever position I held looking for different approaches that would help me to perform my responsibilities more effectively. My approach was to discover an interesting idea that worked for another business, morph it into something different that would work for my organization and implement it with passion, tenacity and perseverance. I dubbed my approach *constructive emulation*: innovation by learning, discovery, adaptation and relentless execution.

In this spirit of constructive emulation, I hope that you enjoy the experience of reading my material, and become excited by the ideas presented and highly motivated to implement them in a way that works for you. I don't intend that the Be Different theme of this book be prescriptive in any sense. I'm not suggesting that my ideas will be the panacea for your organization's ills. Rather, I trust that the ideas which benefited businesses and organizations for me will do the same for you.

Constructive Emulation: innovation by learning, discovery, adaptation and relentless execution.

Feel free to modify an idea to meet the very special circumstances of your organization. Launch the implementation process with all the energy, tenacity and passion that you need to lead change in your business. If you rise to the challenge, then I will consider my experience to have made a difference.

My book is presented in five sections. The first deals with the business context for *BE DiFFERENT* and why it is an important survival tool for any organization today. The next four sections examine Be Different opportunities in the areas of strategic or business planning, marketing, sales, and serving customers. At the end of each section I summarize the main themes discussed as *Learning Points* to serve as a reminder and to reinforce the material covered. In most chapters, *Quick Hits* are provided to recap the ideas presented in the chapter but with a different emphasis and perspective to aid the learning process.

You can read the book from cover to cover to experience the flow and continuity of the material or you can pick a chapter that intrigues you and begin there. I hope you then return to the sections that have the greatest potential to help your organization.

I trust that *BE DiFFERENT or be dead* will be an important reference source and an ongoing guide to refresh the ideas you learn, keep them alive, and provide continuous value to you.

Read on, and enjoy the ride!

Section One

BE DiFFERENT Strategic Imperative

Chapter One

In 2008 the forestry industry in British Columbia was in the tank. Export markets were drying up as the strength of the Canadian dollar made it more difficult for companies to compete in the U.S. marketplace.

In addition, forestry companies saw margins shrink as sales declined without commensurate reductions in operating expenses. The profitability of most companies in this sector was at best marginal; at worst, it was non-existent. Many businesses failed. Furthermore, many of these were well-established firms well known on the international stage for their quality products and services.

It couldn't Be Different so it is dead. Not a unique situation, but one where an organization was unable to respond to an external body blow.

One example was a company on Vancouver Island in business for a number of years successfully manufacturing and selling new equipment as well as providing parts and service to its customers. It went into receivership. Factors that contributed to its vulnerability to an economic downturn included the following:

- The bread and butter business for this company was new equipment sales to both Canadian and U.S. markets on the West

1

Coast; with the downturn of the forestry sector it saw its revenue go into free fall.

- It had, as a result, a huge inventory of these new machines available with no purchasers in sight.

- A handful of customers in both Canadian and U.S. markets generated a disproportionate amount of its revenue.

This company was unable to adapt to changing market conditions. The downturn in the forestry sector did not appear overnight. The company could have been aware, in light of this, that the loss of new equipment sales would mean plummeting profit margins. Looking at common business performance indicators, it could have changed its strategy to minimize the potential negative impacts.

The organization's survival was at risk and the indicators were clear. It was simply not capable of immunizing itself. Management, mindlessly devoted to manufacturing and selling new equipment even when there was no market for it, was unable to change direction quickly and focus on the profitable parts and service business, driving operating expenses out and morphing the company to Be Different from its competitors. As a result it failed.

Unpredictable events challenge traditional business management techniques; the application of old thinking is a recipe for disaster.

My Be Different strategic imperative is based on the reality that most organizations today operate in a world of unpredictability, constantly challenged by random events that test their viability. In such an environment, organizations must develop a business strategy based on the market dynamics most likely to affect them. And they must react fast when planning assumptions fail to materialize.

The forestry example above makes the point: the company may not have been able to predict the economic downturn in their markets but once management became aware of declining financial performance, it could have changed its business strategy to minimize the potential negative impacts.

In today's volatile environment, random external events challenge the traditional techniques used to manage them. Many businesses, however, still rely almost exclusively on traditional forecasting tools and models to predict where they will be in the future, leaving little room for these unexpected events. Exclusive use of these tools to predict business outcomes could be a recipe for disaster.

We can count on facing predictable uncertainty at an accelerating pace, causing organizational discontinuity.

You simply cannot assume that the future will be an extension of the past. To do so would suggest that past successes will determine future wins. In an all-things-remaining-equal environment you might be able to get away with this. But the fact is that as a business looks forward in time, all things are not equal. The only thing we can count on is facing uncertainty at an accelerating pace with significant impact on our organizations. The events in the market worldwide in the past several months demonstrate this clearly.

I am not suggesting that predictive tools and methodologies do not play a valuable role in business. They do. They offer one version of an outcome. But that outcome may be wrong. We have all seen how unexpected forces in the market cause that outcome to fall short of expectations.

Think of the trend line version of your future as a baseline view from which you need to be prepared to move when things start to go haywire. I admit that in the rarest of circumstances a random event may create a windfall for a company; when it does, rejoice. And then prepare yourself for a shock that will take you in the opposite direction.

Successful organizations understand the need to learn from the past and apply that learning to future scenarios. They also know that they must lead into an uncertain future by introducing new ideas, concepts and tools to prevent organizational mortality. Those that don't, continue to toil on in the mistaken belief that the actions behind past successes will continue to work in the future. This *momentum management* results in the demise of organizations. The issue is not whether it will happen, but when.

What are the key external factors that challenge business success and long term sustainability? Here are some of the key ones that I have observed.

Momentum management results in the demise of organizations. The issue is not whether it will happen, but when.

Increasingly Demanding Customers

Customers are more demanding than ever before. And they have a right to be. This is not new but is increasing in pace, visibility and impact on businesses in general. Customers today have more choices available to them than ever before, provided by a glut of suppliers in the marketplace. And they have more information than ever before on which to base their choices. Fuelled to a significant degree by the World Wide Web, customers now feel empowered. They have high expectations and will rightfully fight to get what they've been promised.

This customer empowerment is being driven not only by more competitive alternatives and information available to them, but also by mediocre businesses that rarely meet customer expectations. They promise but don't deliver, and nothing is worse than creating expectations and failing to deliver the promised results. When was the last time you purchased something that didn't work the way you were told it would? Or the last time you were promised that your purchase would be delivered on a specific date and it wasn't?

These mediocre companies abuse customers, but to the Be Different organizations looking for an edge, this represents powerful opportunities. Companies that do actually live up to their promises are viewed as progressive and tend to win in the market. They don't have to be extraordinary. They simply need to find out what customers want and deliver it consistently. Not rocket science, but it works.

Customers feel empowered. They have a right to expect certain things from the companies they do business with and they'll fight to get what they've been promised.

Crazy Competition

It's a tough job for an organization to create and sustain a competitive advantage in the market these days. In addition to increased competition from existing firms, new businesses are being formed at an ever increasing rate. In fact this large and complex competitive mosaic in today's market economy is changing at a blistering pace.

The sources of new competition are numerous compared to previous times:

- The push of new technologies provides new products and services, many of which result in new businesses. Think about the home entertainment sector and the number of new products on the market such as Apple's extremely successful iPod product line. There never seems to be a shortage of technological innovation. However, brilliant technology does not guarantee a successful business. The challenge for companies is to turn a brave technology idea into a thriving business.

- New applications on the Internet are driving a proliferation of competitors. Witness what is happening in the social networking space, for example with MySpace and Facebook, Internet applications that are capturing the imagination of the market.

5

Another relatively new market opportunity made possible by the Internet is online comparison shopping or lead generation; a multimillion dollar a year business whereby operators develop super portals meant to entertain, inform and educate users on certain topics or marketplaces. Go to Google, type in any keyword or combination of keywords and these portals will pop up — contact lenses, laptops, web hosting, health, real estate, education — even online poker, sports betting and bingo! Significant time and expertise is invested in these lead generation portals to ensure that they receive the necessary high ranking in Google to be successful, using features like fresh content, in-depth product or service reviews, unique functionality and, of course, search engine optimization.

The Internet is the mother of new competitor formation.

These are classic referral businesses that generate revenue every time a visitor to their portals clicks out to another website and actually buys something. For businesses looking to Be Different, incorporating these lead generators into your channel mix is a must. Leads are qualified and motivated to purchase — what else do you need?

- Creative market segmentation is exposing new opportunities in smaller, more unique market clusters. Meals for Mums Delivery Inc. (www.mealsformums.com), a Vancouver-based company launched in 2008, decided to target the 'new Moms' market niche. These innovators saw an opportunity to solve the problem that new mothers face for the first few weeks they are at home with their babies. They are so busy taking care of their infants they have no time to eat healthfully themselves. Meals for Mums prepares and delivers healthy pre-cooked meals to mothers, meeting a need that no one else addresses. Clever and impressive, this company represents an excellent example of identifying a small unserviced market segment and exploiting it.

Another terrific example of a recently formed company is TheJobMagnet Interactive Inc., which was founded to address the difficulty companies in the retail and hospitality industries have in attracting new employees, particularly part-time workers. These employers generally advertise in places such as online job boards and want ads which don't attract the usual service industry applicants.

TheJobMagnet decided to solve this by leveraging social networking sites such as Facebook, getting potential workers to fill out job applications for these entry-level retail and hospitality sectors. These applications are then made available to employers who pay a fee for each candidate who applies for a job. This is an impressive example of a company that turned a very real human resource problem into a new market opportunity by using the power of the Internet.

- In an effort to build shareholder value, businesses are creating sub-businesses that can be separated to compete on their own. For example, a few years ago Air Canada decided to spin off Aeroplan, its frequent flier program, to compete free from the influences of its parent company.

Another example is the recent plan to split the energy giant, EnCana, into its two key components: natural gas production and oil sands operations. *The Globe and Mail* described the move as another dramatic act of self-destruction, a concept originated by the Austrian-born economist Joseph Schumpeter, who put forward the notion that capitalist societies are in a perpetual state of creative destruction. I think this is a great description for the seemingly natural process that businesses go through to free-up value, creating a more focused competitive strategic direction for their component parts. The EnCana proposal would present a formidable threat to two of its competitors, Canadian Natural Resources Ltd. and Nexen Inc., who would have to consider the challenges to them by more focused competition from the two new EnCana businesses.

The challenge for any organization in an environment where new businesses are constantly being created is to be nimble on its feet and adapt as competitive complexity increases, as well as to have a clear understanding of its unique value in the market and why it should be the supplier of choice.

Fickleness Trumps Loyalty

Today, achieving a high level of customer loyalty is almost becoming the impossible dream. Organizations face the reality that, after investing heavily to acquire customers, those same customers will leave them in a heartbeat when a better offer comes along. It wasn't always like this. In the past, customers faced stronger barriers to exit when it came to switching suppliers. These barriers included such things as lack of information on competitive alternatives, fewer choices, monopoly supply and technology.

Today, customers will leave you in a heartbeat for a better offer when value isn't unique.

Customers today, however, find it relatively easy to change service providers; the risks of doing so are low as well. This customer churn challenge for any organization is fuelled by:

- Greater technological compatibility enabling a customer to change suppliers without losing the basic functionality they have. Moving from one computer manufacturer to another, for example, has little risk associated with it in terms of not being able to run program applications that you regularly use or maintaining your data files in the new operating environment.

- Marketing programs offering strong economic incentives for a customer to change suppliers. The delight of telemarketers, you see these all the time. 'Switch from company A for your service to us and receive three months free service' is not an uncommon sales proposition, enticing people to consider competitive options. I find it interesting that few such propositions offer value-based reasons for switching. If I come to you for three free months' service today, what makes you think I won't leave you in three months for the same or better offer? In the early days of long distance competition we had a list of customers we called 'switchers' who constantly changed telecom carriers to take advantage of offers like these.

Too Much Competitive Chatter

More competition and the accelerating rate of new business formation have resulted in more advertising and media clutter than ever before. Inundated with sales propositions, we are nevertheless left on our own to interpret what is being said to us and to decide which company can best serve our specific needs.

Few companies provide prospective customers with simple, clear value-based reasons to buy from them and no one else. Little is said about their products and services or their customer and after-sales service. On the other hand, these firms bring out the guns when it relates to offering price-related reasons to join them. The newspapers are full of ads highlighting 50% off, the lowest prices in town, no payments until 2010 and 'we pay the sales tax for the month of March.' If the bad news from a business survival point of view is that price tends to be used as the silver bullet, the good news is if an organization can discover a value niche, it will be the long term winner.

Rules. Rules. Rules.

There are many external bodies in the marketplace that play a major role in determining the future of an organization. These consist of government or quasi-government agencies with mandates such as protecting consumer rights, ensuring there is a level playing field in competitive markets, setting minimum wage levels for employees, maintaining cultural standards, establishing safe workplace practices and effectively deploying scarce technological resources, to name a few.

Sales pitches rain down on us relentlessly, and we are left to filter them to find those that meet our needs.

Regulation, specifically, plays a major role as a chaos driver these days because regulatory outcomes can have a significant impact on an organization's ability to both attract and hold its customers. It can dramatically impact your organization and you have minimal ability to anticipate or control it in most cases. It is a matter of a quick response and a clear direction that will ensure your survival.

To illustrate this point, consider some of the regulatory decisions rendered over the last twenty to twenty-five years in the spirit of encouraging more competition in the telecommunications market in Canada. As you read the following examples, imagine the potential vulnerability that each regulatory event placed on the incumbent telecom companies and the responses that were necessary to satisfy shareholders. Ask yourself how many other sectors had to take this many *right angled turns* in their approach to the market in order to continue to be successful?

- The decision to permit terminal attachment in the early 1980s to compete with the provincial telephone companies supplying telephone equipment essentially eliminated the historical telephone monopoly and opened up the industry to many new competitors as well as intense price competition. Interestingly, the regulatory promise of technological and new product innovation for customers was never completely fulfilled, given that most of the new telephone equipment competitors were really distributors and that most product innovation was driven by equipment manufacturers such as Nortel, Mitel and GTE. The promise of lower prices to consumers, on the other hand, was realized from the new telephone suppliers, as most chose to compete by offering lower prices rather than better value.

- A regulatory decision that had an even greater impact on telephone companies in both Canada and the U.S. resulted in opening up the long distance business to competition. As over 50% of most telephone carriers' revenue came from long distance service at that time, this decision clearly placed the incumbents at significant financial risk.

- In both the terminal attachment and long distance decisions the carriers had to file tariffs for new services and adjust prices due to market forces. The new competitors, however, were allowed the freedom to introduce new services and to set prices at, or change prices to, any level they wanted without regulatory oversight. For the telephone companies, this caused significant delays in introducing new services to the market as well as in making any pricing adjustments that were required due to competitive activities.

Regulation is a chaos driver for business; regulatory outcomes can dramatically impact the performance of an organization.

- Additional constraints on the incumbent telephone companies to compete in long distance services included the rule that stipulated if the company lost a long distance customer to a competitor, it could not try to win back that customer for a certain period of time. This policy was intended to give new entrants the advantage of cementing a relationship with customers while giving them time to become established and remain viable.

- More recently, the regulator continued to intervene in the telecom sector. Allowing customers to change their mobility suppliers while keeping their original phone numbers, referred to as number portability, eliminated one of the main switching costs for customers. Changing telephone numbers with a change in mobility provider was inconvenient and, for business customers, a costly proposition. This regulatory policy change made it easy for people to switch to an alternative mobility supplier and threaten the incumbent.

- In 2008, Industry Canada, the custodian of Canada's wireless spectrum, awarded 40% of new spectrum to a number of new entrants with a $4.25 billion windfall for the federal government. As a result there will probably be one more national wireless competitor and between two and five new provincial competitors. Lots of interest in the $16 billion wireless market in Canada; more challenges for the existing wireless suppliers to respond to a rather far-reaching government policy change. Hang on, shareholders!

My point in outlining the regulatory history of the telecom business is not to whine about the injustice and unreasonableness of the decisions taken. Rather, the point is that, despite exhaustive, lengthy and costly involvement on the part of the telecom companies, regulatory decisions were made that substantially increased financial risk and caused the companies to dramatically change the way they conducted their business. Not a bad thing necessarily, but an example of a series of external events that drove an entire industry to constantly reinvent itself in order to survive forces beyond its control.

Finally, a Statistics Canada study by John R. Baldwin entitled *Failing Concerns: Business Bankruptcy in Canada* supports the above factors as contributing to the failure of a business. Even though the study is a decade old, its conclusions certainly resonate with the challenges businesses are facing in the current economic meltdown. Baldwin concludes that firms fail because of both unanticipated external shocks and internal deficiencies.

The study found that the top six *external causes* of business failure were:

1. Economic downturn in the market facing the firm (the forestry sector, for example)

2. Increased competition

3. Customer difficulties — loss of a major customer as the result of relocation or market change

4. Fundamental change in market conditions

5. Government regulation

6. Fundamental change in technology

A single factor alone doesn't kill a business; a number of factors collaborate to produce the destructive perfect storm.

It concluded that it is unlikely that there is a single factor alone that kills a business; rather, it is more likely that a number of factors collaborate to produce the destructive perfect storm. The forestry example earlier in the chapter illustrates this point: the economy was poor, the company's competitiveness was declining and it had a small number of customers generating a disproportionate amount of sales volume.

However, the study goes on to say that almost half of the firms in Canada that go bankrupt fail primarily because of their own internal deficiencies rather than these externally generated problems alone. In other words, faced with external unforeseen pressures, businesses fail because they are not able internally to figure out how to react to them and survive.

The most significant *internal deficiencies* cited were:

1. Inability to adapt to change

2. Lack of flexibility and initiative

3. Poor communication

4. Lack of organizational vision and planning

5. Lack of marketing

Addressing these organizational skills is certainly necessary to build business value in good times; they are absolutely critical to survival in bad times. My Be Different strategies will show you how.

QUICK HITS

- A major cause of business failure is due to unforeseen external factors such as economic downturn, increasing competition, outrageous demands from customers, increasing disloyalty of customers, the loss of a small number of customers that generate a disproportionately large amount of revenue, technological change and government regulation.

- External factors alone, however, don't kill businesses; how organizations respond to unpredictable external shocks is a major determinant of whether or not they survive.

- Among the major internal deficiencies that cause failure are the inability of the organization to adapt to tumultuous change, lack of marketing skills and the lack of organizational vision and planning.

- An organization needs a strategic plan that is based on the best available information that its leadership team has; however, in order to adapt to unforeseen events, the plan needs to be modified on a moment's notice in favor of a new direction when external events dictate.

Chapter Two

If business failure is due in large part to the lack of organizational survival skills, what's the solution? How do you develop these skills? What are the things that an organization should do to immunize itself against the shocks of external events?

The answer can be boiled down to this: If you are not *different* you are dead or you soon will be. In other words, to be able to survive, an organization needs to position itself uniquely in the marketplace. It must be able to carve out a special place in the customer's mind so that loyalty is not only created but also has a long life. An organization must Be Different.

If you're not different you are dead or soon will be.

I'm sure you've heard it said that if the external environment is changing faster than the inside of an organization, the end is near. You need to recognize and keep pace with the dynamics impacting your business, and if you fail to do so, it will not be a question of whether or not your organization will die; it will be a matter of when.

Brian Canfield, a former CEO of BC Telecom, was exceptional at reading the signs of the time. He accurately identified the regulatory changes that would dramatically alter the face of telecommunications in Canada and pose significant economic challenges to the incumbent telephone companies. He also predicted that there would be a consolidation of the players in the industry in order to achieve the scale and scope necessary to successfully compete and grow. He was right on this point as well. A leader like Brian, with an intuitive sense for future events, is critical to the next step: preparing the organization to be different and survive.

The interesting thing is that you don't necessarily have to be better than your competitors; you just have to be different. I am not suggesting that you can get away with providing shoddy products and services or marginal customer service; rather that you find a way to redefine yourself as different from others in the marketplace and give customers what they want in the quality they expect.

You don't have to be better. You have to Be Different.

The challenge is to create meaningful and compelling differences that will separate you from your competition, and to articulate these differences to your target customers in a way that will convince them to do business with your organization and no one else. A meaningful difference is value, provided that it combines a high *must matter* factor to the customer with a *low currently satisfied* factor. It is something that is really important to the customer and is currently not satisfied by any supplier in the market.

You need to get the customer's attention, clear the message clutter, and then tell them in very clear and specific terms why they only have one choice, and that choice is you. This process requires that your organization develop and communicate a value proposition to the market that is truly unique.

QUICK HITS

■ In order to survive chaotic market forces, an organization needs to create relevant and compelling reasons why customers should buy from them.

■ Organizations that are not successful in cutting through the communications clutter in the marketplace to distinguish themselves from their competition are either dead now or they will be very soon.

■ *Be Different* or be dead. The key to business survival.

Chapter Three

If you were to scrutinize closely the value propositions being advertised by organizations these days, you would find generally two categories: those that use price as the way to distinguish themselves from their competition, and those that use non-price, or value reasons to separate. The Be Different approach is that value differences are the only meaningful ones, and indeed they are the only differences that will give your business the ability to survive in the long run. Think about it this way. Value is the immunization factor that will help to avoid the decline and eventual demise of your business.

So, what is value? Well, it is a continuum that represents the relationship between price and another business variable. Here are some examples:

Price ————————————— x ————————→ Product Quality

Price ———————— x —————————————→ Fashionability

Price ————————————————— x ——→ Service

Price —x ——————————————————→ Location

Price ——————————————————— x → Brand

Value in the first instance is significantly weighted toward the quality of the product being offered, the indicators that the market is willing to pay a higher price for a quality product. In the second example, on the other hand, customers are willing to pay less for the fashion aspects of a product. The third example indicates that higher levels of service draw more premium prices than do lower levels of service. The fourth and fifth examples illustrate that customers aren't willing to pay much for the location of the supplier but the brand is able to pull higher prices. If you understood these price–value relationships, which value component would you consider incorporating into your core business strategy and be prepared to invest in?

If an organization cannot come up with meaningful and compelling value differences to separate itself from its competition, then price will be the only differentiating factor between you and your competitors. For example, if you and your competitors all claim to be the best provider of fashion clothing but customers cannot perceive any difference among the fashion products offered, then the competition will tend to gravitate over time to price as the main differentiator.

Value is the immunization factor. When there is no difference in value people buy on price alone.

The problem with depending on a price strategy is twofold. First, having a price edge is not sustainable; others can easily copy it and they will. Second, if you decide to compete on price, you are placing your organization in a very challenging economic position. Constant cost pressure will keep you awake at night as margins are squeezed due to prices moving down.

I am not saying that you can't compete successfully in the commodity space. Many companies that use price as their primary differentiator are also looking for non-price factors that will help keep them from becoming a pure price play. The big box retailers, for example, try to lever their brands, range of products, convenient locations, etc. to shed the commodity image. Nevertheless, the fact remains that they compete largely on price. For smaller businesses without the economies of scale and scope of these large organizations, the commodity game is a tough one to win.

When you decide to compete on value, you can develop a strategy that will be very difficult for your competitors to copy. They may not have the required technology, at least for a time, or the employee expertise or organizational infrastructure necessary to develop the value capabilities required to compete with you. Your competitors' challenge of course is that in order to build these required capabilities they must be prepared to make, in most cases, additional investments in terms of technology, people, systems, etc., requiring additional financial resources. Many would not be prepared to do so.

Competing on value allows you to create a Be Different strategy that your competitors will have difficulty copying.

The value differences you create are not only the barriers your competitors face in deciding to enter your market space. They are also the reasons why your customers will stay loyal to you. Your competition will think long and hard about trying to compete with you and in most cases will tend to go where fruit is hanging low rather than make large investments to get a piece of your action. And, if they do decide to compete with you, they will most likely offer lower prices as the way to attract your customers. This tactic won't succeed in any event because the value shield you provide your customers will keep them from leaving and will block competitors at your gates. Value beats price any day.

QUICK HITS

■ Be Different organizations compete on unique value attributes that are demanded by the market and represent core competencies that they have but others don't.

■ Organizations that cannot define a value that is unique to them end up standing for a range of value attributes that are common to others and trying then to be known for having the lowest price.

■ Having value that is common to your competitors while selling at lower prices is not a long term winning strategy. At some point your lowest price will be matched and your options will be limited.

Chapter Four

The Only Statement: The Birth of Differentiation

Most businesses are doing their best to position themselves as being unique in the market. The problem is, however, that they resort to clichés as opposed to crisp clear differentiation claims that make it easy for customers to separate them from the crowd. Such claims as we provide the best service, we provide the highest quality products, we are the supplier of choice, we've been in business for thirty years and we are the most trusted organization are examples of statements that are trying to carve out a unique competitive position but fail to do so.

Consider these typical responses from Canadian businesses who answered the question, 'What are you offering to your customers that sets you apart from the competition?'

- 'We… have been doing business here for nearly three decades. Offering quality products, great prices and excellent service in an easy-access location is definitely the foundation to our success.' — a carpet company

- 'We have very low prices on the exact same products you would find at a big box retail store.' — a furniture supplier

- 'In addition to having a great selection of frames and lenses, we provide top-notch service.' — a supplier of glasses

- 'We have been in business a long time, and are fortunate to have lots of regular customers, we buy with their tastes in mind, exceptional customer service, two unique discount programs.' — a clothing store

- 'We've got great, fresh simple homemade fare from local B.C. ingredients, warm atmosphere, live entertainment and dancing.' — a restaurant

- 'Utmost in service and selection, fit is crucial.' — a shoe company

- 'Helpful friendly professionals who enjoy assisting patients. It is their goal to maintain exceptional service as their top priority.' — hearing consultants

- 'Variety of unique and effective programs for weight loss that you won't find anywhere else, certified personal trainer, registered nutritionist on site, work with you one-on-one.' — a weight loss business

Some of these statements aspire to uniqueness at best while others are a little clearer about what sets them apart. Unfortunately, when the claim merely aspires, the message gets lost in the media clutter and people are then left on their own to figure out whether you are in fact different enough to attract their business. Do your customers a favor and make it easy for them to get a clear understanding of how you differ from everyone else out there.

The only statement forces you to consider customer benefits that only you provide; aspirations do nothing but make you feel good.

How does an organization know whether or not it has meaningful value differences to offer existing and prospective customers? One method of answering this question is to compose what I call the *only* statement for your organization. It is a simple but powerful concept for articulating your uniqueness versus that of your competitors.

It goes like this:

> We are the *only* ones that...

The objective in developing this statement is to define the exclusive value or customer benefits that your organization provides. The use of the word *only* is critical as it forces you to consider the benefits that you alone provide.

The workshop method involving the leaders of the organization is an effective way to try to compose your *only* statement. If you can compose a crystal clear, detailed statement your team has a good understanding of the differentiation game. On the other hand, don't be surprised if the exercise causes you a great deal of pain and agony and you simply cannot complete the task. Do not despair. This is a tough assignment. In fact you may never be able to define your organization as being 100% unique.

After hours of grueling *only* work with your colleagues, you may have to concede that you are currently basically the same as others but you do have the skills to be truly unique if you did something different. If so, develop the competencies to move your business into the Be Different space and communicate it clearly to the market.

BE DiFFERENT or be dead is the only book that offers a practical how to approach to enhance the performance of organizations to ensure they thrive and survive in the long term. The ideas presented here have been tested in the real world and have been successfully implemented across all critical business functions.

If your team believes that your organization is only a three out of ten on the *only* scale, celebrate it. At least you know where you stand and you can now move on. You are better off than the numerous organizations out there that aren't going through this strategic exercise at all.

I want to note here that you don't have to be a large organization to reap the benefits of this approach. In fact, small businesses and single proprietors can, and should, develop the *only* statement for their businesses. All businesses need to distinguish themselves in the market.

In creating this book, I gave a considerable thought to how I was going to position it in the business book market. At first I was overwhelmed by the task, given the competition in the publishing business. There is an abundance of books available by very well known authors all professing to help people improve organizational and personal performance.

Here is my *only* statement for this book:

> *BE DiFFERENT or be dead* is the *only* book that offers a practical how-to approach to enhance the performance of organizations to ensure they thrive and survive in the long term. The ideas presented here have been tested in the real world and have been successfully implemented across all critical business functions.

If a company is different it should scream its difference in advertising.

It's a challenge to identify more than a handful of organizations that have explicitly developed the *only* statement. A principal source for this information would be strategy documentation which is held to be confidential by most companies. But the other source, which is a more relevant one, is the advertising material an organization uses in the market. In fact, if a company really believes it is different it should be expressing that difference in the advertising it develops and presents to customers.

My research of companies that explicitly use the *only* statement produced the following examples.

Queen's School of Business (www.business.queensu.ca) is located in Kingston, Ontario, and is rated number one in Canada for its full-time MBA program. The school advertises aggressively to attract candidates to its program. Here is some advertising copy I have seen:

'Queen's Full-Time MBA is one of the world's premier MBA programs, renowned for its leading-edge curriculum and innovative approaches to learning. But what really sets it apart is its focus on you. Only Queen's provides personal development coaching to build on your individual strengths, as well as specialized electives tailored to your specific career aspirations, in order to help you achieve the greatest personal and professional growth.

Business is a team sport. And like any sport, it takes practice. At Queen's you will be assigned to a student team for the core of the program, enabling you to develop and sharpen the team and leadership skills that are so critical to success today.'

Queen's positioning statement is impressive. First of all, it separates itself from all the other MBA program providers by providing personal coaching to focus on the special needs of each and every student. The implication is that no other business school applies standard programs across the entire student body, catering to the personal needs of the individual. Secondly, in the last paragraph of the quote, the Queen's offer highlights the team involvement in enhancing the student's team and leadership skills necessary in business. Queen's is not only positioning its MBA program as unique — the *only* statement — but also as extremely relevant in terms of preparing students for the world of business in areas of interpersonal relations, conflict management and leadership. I also have the impression that it is the only organization that provides this type of learning. Excellent work.

Queen's separates itself from other MBA programs by providing personal coaching to meet the special needs of each student.

As Senior VP Marketing for BC Telecom, I devised and negotiated a deal with ADT Home Security to offer a service package consisting of telecom and security services for the residential consumer. In our promotional material we positioned this package as '... exclusively for BC Tel customers'. This exclusive position is an indirect way of using the *only* statement, as you could say 'We are the only communications company in B.C. that offers home security and home telephone services in one simple package. In fact I like this better than the exclusive reference. It is a cleaner, far more effective statement.

Whrrl (www.whrrl.com) is a location-based social utility service, offered by the Seattle-based company Pelago, that helps people answer questions like 'Where should we go for dinner tonight?' or 'What leisure activities can I do around here?' whether you are in your home town or traveling. The service is positioned as a unique solution using the Internet to answer personal but general questions that are difficult to answer through common Internet search engines. In response to general questions like this, search engines typically produce information that is vague or irrelevant. Whrrl organizes everything you and your friends know about people, places and events and puts that information at your fingertips! The intent of Whrrl is to create for each customer '… a social discovery experience that combines the power of the Internet with the dead-on trustworthiness and fun of getting recommendations from friends.' Whrrl creates a personal community of information tailored to the unique tastes and preferences for each user of the service with information from friends, family and other approved contacts.

Whrrl's *only* statement is found in a quote from Jeff Holden, the co-creator of the service:

> 'We're trying to help people discover things that there is basically no way to do today.'

My version of this, based on the information I have read, would say:

> Whrrl is the *only* service that combines Internet search capabilities with personal recommendations from friends to allow someone to discover activities in their social community that are personally relevant and meaningful.

AM 730 Radio in Vancouver (CHMJ), part of the Corus Entertainment Inc. Vancouver radio cluster of stations, has a very clean approach to positioning itself through the use of the *only* statement. Here is what one of the station's print ads says:

> 'AM 730, All Traffic All the Time. AM 730 Vancouver's Traffic Station is the only station providing traffic twenty-four hours a day seven days a week. AM 730's weekly audience has grown over 500% since launching, and more and more people are saving time and money by listening every day.'

This *only* position was created by the Vancouver Corus team who were looking for a replacement format to their all-sports station MOJO 730. Not only was MOJO number two in the market at the time, it was losing millions of dollars annually. The solution the team came up with was to establish an all-traffic format that is literally the only one of its kind in the world! And in less than twenty-four months the new station was profitable.

AM 730, Vancouver's only 24/7 traffic station, also blocked competition for a sister station.

In addition, I found the strategic fit of this all-traffic format with the other stations in the cluster — News Talk 980, Alternative Rock CFOX and Classic Rock 101 — particularly clever and well executed. According to J.J. Johnston, General Manager of Corus Vancouver, 'AM 730 works as an effective blocker for our premium station CKNW News Talk 980 against our prime competitor News 1130 which has had it traffic position severely impaired.'

So the Corus innovation resulted in a Be Different double whammy. They carved out a truly unique niche for AM 730 and integrated it into their station cluster in a way that builds the performance of its flagship CKNW station. Nice. Congratulations, Corus Vancouver team.

Canadian Imperial Bank of Commerce (CIBC), one of Canada's largest banks, advertises one of its newest loyalty card products this way:

> 'The only infinite card made from pure gold.'

The ad goes on to list the features of this unique card in this way:

- 1.5 air miles for every dollar spent on gas, grocery and drugstores

- Extended privileges at select hotels and restaurants, free

- Prestige of travel concierge service, free

- Peace of mind of 15-day travel medical insurance, free'

It is interesting to note that CIBC chose to take an *only* position in additional air miles and other services a cardholder gets with this card, whereas other banks, who also market a similar card, use different approaches.

TD Canada Trust, for example, claims uniqueness by stating in its advertising:

'Unlike other points cards, we let you book any way you want.'

It goes on to say:

'The new TD First Class Travel Infinite Card is making it easier than ever to get the trip you want using TD Points. Unlike other cards, it could be a trip you book on a travel website, through a travel agent, or a seat sale with any airline.'

In other words TD is saying that it is the only bank that understands how difficult it is at times to book travel using card points, and it has created a unique card to relieve the frustration. I really like TD's approach! I think it is clever to make its only claim around solving a very real problem that many people experience every day! Only with our card can you solve a very real problem. Brilliant.

In the center of downtown Vancouver, there are 25 exclusive homes being marketed by Sotheby's and the Delta Group.

The property is named The Private Residences at Hotel Georgia (www.residencesatgeorgia.com); the full page ad goes like this:

'There Will Always ONLY EVER BE ONE… In a market crowded with towers, The Private Residences at Hotel Georgia offer something completely unique that could *ONLY* happen in Vancouver.'

The claim is followed by a number of supporting proof points:

- 'Only One Location Like This' – describing the physical location of the property in the heart of the city '… surrounded by boutiques and gourmet restaurants, this is the most vibrant central location in all of Vancouver. In the heart of the Luxury District, this is truly an exclusive address.'

- 'An Irreplaceable Memory' – describing the Hotel Georgia as 'The hub of Vancouver's social life. All the stars, the Royals, and heads of state stayed here. This is a place with a past that can't be duplicated: the only luxury residences anchored by a significant heritage landmark.'

- 'A Singular Hotel' – suggesting that 'All the best hotels in the world are not part of a chain. They are singular and unique.'

- 'Intelligent Floor Plans' – assuring the reader that floor plans have been designed to simplify your daily life… 'Every floor plan is carefully constructed to make you feel more at home.'

- 'Vancouver's Best Chef' – announcing that 'Your home will be adjoined to the best restaurant in Vancouver with room service if you want, featuring the well-known chef, David Hawksworth.'

- 'Canada's Most Celebrated Interior Designer'

- 'An Experienced Developer'

- 'An Exclusive Alliance With Sotheby's' – suggesting that the Sotheby's name has been synonymous with luxury… 'It represents only the most extraordinary properties such as The Private Residences at Hotel Georgia.'

This is the most robust example of *only* work I found in all my research. It states that the development is unique and then goes on to list individual attributes of The Residences and tries to make the same claim for each of them. While it doesn't succeed in all of them, they make the point successfully in most of them. Nicely done. A good template for others who aspire to the *only* fame.

Earlier, I mentioned a company called TheJobMagnet Interactive Inc. that is exploiting the Internet to make it much more effective for employers to find part-time workers in the retail and hospitality industries. Visit them on www.thejobmagnet.com to see the *only* statement they developed.

> 'Unlike job boards, TheJobMagnet is the *only* pay-for-performance interactive recruiting service that goes where the candidates are, instead of making them find us. Our complete line of interactive candidate sourcing services addresses your recruiting needs, while our success-based pricing ensures you only ever pay for performance, not promises.'

Clear, concise, compelling and expressing a solution to a very real business problem. An awesome example!

A Da Vinci on your wrist: can you imagine it?

Some organizations don't use the *only* statement explicitly, but the messages they convey about their products make the point implicitly. I read an advertisement in a local Vancouver newspaper for Brinkhaus jewelers. The product in the ad was a man's watch, the IWC, which had many characteristics men would find useful, in particular a stopwatch time function which '... is as easy to read as the time of day.' What captured my attention, however, was the tag line for the product which reads:

> 'The best place to put a Da Vinci: on your wrist.'

Given the uniqueness of Leonardo Da Vinci's work and the value of his paintings, the positioning of the watch as an exclusive product to Brinkhaus is very evident. I found this a very effective use of the *only* approach; an excellent example of the indirect method.

■ The Be Different mantra is to be the only one that provides a service or a product in a way that mirrors what customers want.

■ The *only* statement will set your team apart from all the others in the market who are striving to avoid failure; you will be the long term winner.

■ Have some fun with this and get your leadership team together to do the work. You might find that you don't know yourself as well as you think and that what you thought was a strong competitive positioning strategy was more smoke than anything else.

■ Be on the lookout for examples of how others are using the *only* statement to position their organizations. Learn from them; constructively emulate them.

Chapter Five

Let's say that you have constructed the *only* statement for your organization. What next? Should you *boldly* go forward spending mega dollars to communicate it to the world through a multimedia campaign? Not yet. What you really need to do is test your assertions — find out if what you say is relevant and accurate.

Go to your customers (a focus group is a good tool to use for this) to find out, first, whether your *only* statement is compelling. Does it address a need that really matters to your customers? Is it a high priority to them? Does it have a high must-matter factor? Nothing could be worse than going to the market with a claim that doesn't address a high priority customer need.

Do your customers believe your only statement or are you dreaming in the shade?

The second thing you need to find out is if your *only* statement is real. Is it true? Sometimes we are quite presumptuous about our capabilities as an organization, and we can fantasize in grandiose terms. Find out from your customers if they actually believe the *only* statement you have built or if you are just dreaming in the shade. You can't afford to be mesmerized by your own view of yourself. Go ask the experts — your customers. Once you have customer validation of your work, you are on your way.

As a general guideline, keep your customers close to you at all times. You need to constantly be in touch with them to ensure that whatever *only* claims you are making to the market continue to be real as well as a high priority. If your claim is suddenly out of sync with your target customers, your competitors are probably making inroads in your market and you could be in trouble. You should revisit your work often and reinvent your uniqueness.

QUICK HITS

■ Don't think too highly of your work in creating your *only* statement. You may be giving yourself more credit than your customers do. Go and test your work on them to ensure that it matters to them and they think it is real. If your feelings are hurt, good. You are better off and are now in a position to do the Be Different work that will make you a long term winner.

■ Keep checking your *only* statement with your customers to test its validity over time. Don't forget, your competitors aren't sleeping.

Chapter Six

At this point, I want to deal with the widely used organizational improvement tool, benchmarking, because its use has a profound impact on your ability to create a Be Different position for your organization.

Some of you might recall that benchmarking, as promulgated by the Total Quality Management (TQM) movement in the 1980s, is defined as the practice of first determining the organization that is 'Best in Class' with respect to a particular business function, process, product or service and then implementing changes in your organization in order to be like, or copy, it. This is intended to improve your performance and effectiveness in large measure as you move to emulate the company with which you are benchmarking yourself. Another way to look at this is that the best-in-class organization sets the performance bar to which another company aspires, and that company spends much time, energy and resources trying to move closer to this lead company.

My issue with this tool is that if you are the company seeking to improve yourself, the only Be Different result of your efforts is that the gap between you and the benchmarked company narrows over time. Yes, you will get better, but it is relative to your own performance, not to the other company. You will in this instance not achieve a unique position, as you are seeking to be the same. Now, this may not matter if you are benchmarking a company in another industry, for example, or a company that is not a competitor where emulation would allow you to be different from your own competition. But in most instances, organizations tend to benchmark others in the same industry; hence my concern that it is not a productive Be Different tool.

Beware of Benchmarking; use it only to establish the bar high and vault high above it.

If you are going to benchmark, use it to establish the highest bar from which your organization wants to Be Different. If you are going to use this tool to improve your performance at least understand the strategic limitations. Copying is the enemy of being different. If you are going to use benchmarking, use it to create differences, and not to copy.

Here's a suggested step-by-step approach:

1. Determine the aspect of your organization that needs performance improvement. The choice should be consistent with your overall differentiation strategy. For example, let's say your organization has chosen to differentiate itself by leveraging your sales capabilities, and has decided to adopt tools for the sales team that will enable it to improve its performance in customer relationship management (CRM).

2. Evaluate the market to see which organization is best at CRM. Again, I would urge you to consider organizations outside as well as within your industry in order to maximize the effectiveness of your selection. I would start by looking outside your industry. Get out of your business box. Look for CRM perfection and then go inside your industry to compare your findings.

3. Perform an in-depth study of the sales tools they use and how they use them. This becomes your baseline target, or the minimum requirement for you to achieve.

4. Determine how you can morph this best-in-class view into an approach that is truly different, i.e. one that is beyond-best-in-class.

5. Implement the beyond best-in-class sales tools and use them in your organization.

Starbucks Coffee Company declared its intent to start marketing to the younger age segment of the market. The correct thinking here is that it is trying to keep pace with the demographic changes affecting its market (the growing segment presumably is the teen segment). My issue with this action was the attempt to position its strategy as being unique while in reality it appeared to be the result of benchmarking to other organizations that were already actively offering specific menus for this particular group of consumers: Tim Horton's and Second Cup. It's OK to be a fast follower but don't attempt to position yourself as the leader.

___

Be Different is beyond best in class.

___

One way to leverage benchmarking to Be Different is to choose your target competitors and then analyze the areas in which they are successful and how they achieve that success. What do they do that is truly remarkable? Do they use the *only* statement? If so, what do they say? What are the implications for you catching up to them and then catapulting beyond them by being different?

QUICK HITS

■ Benchmarking is OK if you are trying to catch up with another organization that you perceive is the best in an area in which you need to improve. It is not OK as a tool to create uniqueness unless you define the best-in-class performance beyond which you want to vault and, in doing so, be unique.

Chapter Seven

The last point I want to emphasize is to be *bold* in your search for being different. Organizations are inherently rich in opportunity. To create the uniqueness you need to survive, look broadly across all functions and aspects of your business.

Be bold in your quest to Be Different. Look everywhere.

- Your business strategy; execution versus content

- Your customer service and support

- Your markets you chose to serve

- Your approach to sales

- Your employees' expertise

- Your brand

- Your use of information technology capabilities

- Your marketing approach; mass marketing versus one-to-one personalized marketing

- Your technology used to provide products and services

To give you a sense of how some companies have chosen one of the above areas to distinguish themselves, here are some examples.

Have you ever heard of Webkinz? Webkinz is the brainchild of GANZ, a company established in 1950 to provide a selection of gift products worldwide, with headquarters in Toronto, Canada, and other offices located in Los Angeles, Hong Kong and Shanghai. From their website www.webkinz.com: 'Webkinz pets are lovable plush pets that each come with a unique Secret Code. With it, you enter Webkinz World where you can care for your pet, answer trivia, earn KinzCash and play the best kids games on the net.'

Webkinz: a plush toy backed by the power of an Internet experience.

As you know, this market is extremely competitive, but what is different about Webkinz is that the company has defined its product to be much more than the toy itself. It has added an experience dimension that utilizes the power of the Internet. When you purchase your Webkinz toy, you go online, adopt it and register its name which is unique to you and no one else. Here are some examples of the experiences available through its website:

- Arcade – games to play

- Clinic – if your Webkinz gets sick visit Dr Quack

- Clubhouse – go here to play with other Webkinz World members (this section has very impressive tools to ensure that a child is not exposed to inappropriate conversation and material)

- Curio Shop – 'Arte Fact is the Curio Shop owner. He's got LOTS of cool stuff on sale all the time.'

- My Room – create a home environment for the toy: the layout of each room of the house, the paint color used in each room and the style of furniture used in each room

- My Pets – see each pet's status, read their bio and reprint their adoption certificate

This approach is impressive. Here is a company that has chosen to provide a product that could be thought of as a commodity, yet has created product attributes that leverage a tool, the Internet, into which its customers are growing in order to differentiate itself. Is it the low price supplier in the market? Not even close.

The Spaghetti Factory in Whistler, British Columbia, is an organization that surprised me in terms of behaving in a Be Different manner. Certainly you would not define this business as a high-end specialty restaurant; it is rather a family-oriented place to go for good food and you don't have to take out a second mortgage on your house to afford it. In addition, you wouldn't typically have expected knock-your-socks-off service. Now I am not sure if it is their strategy per se, but I do know that their approach to serving customers does place this organization in a special class onto themselves.

My experience is not unique but illustrates my point well. Our family of six dined there one evening. We all ordered our food which for one person included a steak done 'medium'. When the food came we discovered that the steak was overdone and sent it back to the kitchen to have another one cooked as requested. The rest of us finished our meals and our steak lover waited. And waited. And waited. Finally the server brought another steak and apologized for the delay. The server then proceeded to tell us that the restaurant would cover the entire bill as a result of the mistake.

The Spaghetti Factory in Whistler: amazing service and an act that I have never found elsewhere. I talk about it constantly.

Now what made this a Be Different experience, since many restaurants will provide a complimentary meal to replace one that has been unacceptable to the customer, was that they wrote off the entire bill: all of the food and, more impressively, all of the beverages including the wine. In a later chapter in the Serving Customers section of this book, we will discuss the concept of service recovery, which is defined as responding to a service breakdown by fixing the problem (in this case replacing the well-done steak with the medium one that was requested in the first place) and then doing the unexpected (covering the entire bill for my family).

ARA Safety Inc. in Vancouver is another company that has chosen to Be Different through the product they offer. They are in the fire prevention and response business with their flagship product the FIT, or Fire Intervention Technology device. This product (view the video showing its operation at www.arasafety.com) is tossed into a room that is totally engulfed in flames, for example, and it knocks the fire down in minutes without destroying the room environment as is often the case when water is used. The point is, no other organization offers this product (that I am aware of) which gives it the early market advantage.

ARA Safety in Vancouver: a product that destroys a fire in minutes. How unique is that?

Rogers Wireless is an excellent example of a company that decided early on to make a network technology decision to Be Different from their Canadian counterparts. Rogers' CEO, Ted Rogers, always the visionary and risk taker, decided to adopt the Global System for Mobile (GSM) technology which was becoming more pervasive throughout the world at that time; his competitors chose to go a different route. Ted's decision was brilliant. GSM not only allows Rogers customers to travel to Europe, for example, and still be able to use their existing mobile phones, it also is the technology platform of choice for suppliers such as Apple who develop innovative wireless devices such as the iPhone. By virtue of having a GSM-based network, Rogers was the first wireless company in Canada to offer a number of innovative new phones, including the Motorola Razr, Sony Walkman Phone, RIM Blackberry Pearl and now the iPhone; an advantage in this extremely fast-growing market they are likely to have until their competition makes the substantial investment required to implement a similar network technology.

Again, in the area of serving customers, Rodeo Jewellers of Vancouver really stands out as a small company that believes in cultivating intimate relationships with their clients and then doing whatever necessary to take care of and dazzle them. Unfortunately, in my experience, customer service generally is not all that memorable regardless of the company you are dealing with. Rodeo Jewellers, though, has definitely got it right.

Personal story: my wife and I have been buying from them for a number of years now and the experience never varies. Their product is always of superb quality, prices are always negotiated (and always end up as a win-win), and as we walk into a meeting with Rita, one of the owners, to review the progress of customizing a piece of jewelry that they are making, our favorite Starbuck's coffee awaits.

Amazing. But there is always an unexpected twist to the service we get. The latest and most memorable event occurred as Rita was making a new wedding band for my wife. It was being designed after one that was in their showcase (and was more expensive than the one we wanted) and would take four or five weeks to complete, which we didn't have a problem with. As we were then getting set to go on vacation for her birthday, my wife would have liked to have the band ready to wear, but really wasn't bothered since she knew that it would take about five weeks to make (managing expectations anyone?).

Rodeo Jewellers in Vancouver: loaning jewelry with no deposit: brilliant service or insanity?

Imagine our surprise when Rita called two days before our departure and offered her the wedding band in their showcase to wear for the sixteen days we would be away. Just come in and pick it up. And, of course, there was no need to put some sort of collateral up in case the ring gets lost or damaged.

Why would she suggest such a thing? Because Rita felt bad that my wife would not have her wedding band while on vacation (even though she had no expectations of having it). Brilliant. Being Different.

The good news is that there are definitely some organizations who are attempting to uniquely position themselves in their markets to successfully compete. The bad news in my view, however, is that we need more of them trying to do it.

QUICK HITS

■ Don't have your blinders on when you look to Be Different.

■ Look at what matters to the customers that you intend to serve.

■ Look at the competencies that your organization currently has.

■ Look at the competencies that customers want and your competitors lack.

■ Look across your organization to discover the Be Different nuggets that either you have or can create to be memorable in your customers' eyes and earn their business for a lifetime.

■ Study how others do it and leapfrog over them.

✓ Today, businesses operate in a world of unpredictability, constantly bombarded by external events that simply cannot be managed in a traditional sense. Yes, you need to be proactive and build a strategy based on the likelihood of certain future events occurring, but you also need to be prepared to renew your business fast by responding to shocks that you have not predicted.

✓ What are the market dynamics that pose significant challenges for businesses today?

- Outrageous customers – Beware of empowered customers. They have more information at their disposal to make product choices and they have more suppliers from which to choose. In addition, the lackluster performance of many organizations is fuelling customer dissatisfaction and consequently providing the motivation for them to flex their muscles.

- Fickle customers – Customers change their minds now more than ever by changing suppliers more frequently, as the costs to a client to switch suppliers are declining and customers display their dissatisfaction and complain with their feet.

- Competitor proliferation – Competitors are springing up all over. The Internet is one driving force that is producing a mosaic of new businesses; constructive self-destruction is another strategy that is creating many businesses from a single one.

- Too much talking – There is an amazing amount of communications clutter in the marketplace, making it extremely difficult for customers to figure out who will best satisfy their needs.

- Government oversight – Regulatory and other government policy changes can impose body blows to an organization which, in turn, must react to these unexpected events and recover from the potential negative impacts on them.

- Technological change – New technologies can render your business obsolete overnight. You need to be on a constant technology watch for you and your competitors.

✓ The prescription to immunize your organization against external shocks and be successful amidst constant and accelerating change is to build a strategic approach that is driven by the need to Be Different from your competitors. If you can't Be Different you are dead, or soon will be.

✓ Competitive differentiation based on unique value differences rather than price differences around common sets of values is the theme of the surviving business. Having the lowest prices on the same products offered by your competitors is not a sustainable position as they can easily copy your prices. Having unique value on some dimension that only you provide, such as service, brand, location, etc., on the other hand, enables you to charge premium prices and achieve sustainable differentiation in the market. Do whatever it takes to avoid commoditization of your business.

✓ The ultimate goal of a Be Different strategy is the ability of an organization to compose the *only* statement for itself. 'We are the *only* ones that…' is a claim that will define your organization's uniqueness. Spell it out and then test it constantly with customers to make sure it is compelling and real and continues to be so.

✓ Beware of benchmarking as a strategy development tool. Benchmarking is useful to determine a path of operational improvement for your business, but it has limitations in helping you to Be Different. Don't benchmark to copy the best-in-class company. Benchmark to establish the baseline level of performance you want to exceed.

✓ Opportunities abound in any organization to Be Different. Look at every aspect you offer to customers and how you do it. Evaluate all of your organizational capabilities and look for ways to leverage them, distinguishing yourself from the pack. Check out Webkinz; they know how to do it.

Section Two

BE DiFFERENT Business Strategy

2

Section Introduction

Why is a Be Different strategy important and how do you develop one?

First of all, you need to look at every possible aspect of your organization to be different and a business strategy is a very good place to start. If your business strategy is different everything that flows from that strategy will reflect that difference and your chances for survival and success improve exponentially. A business strategy applies to all areas of your organization, including marketing, sales and customer service.

All strategies are inherently flawed in their essence; few have a unique intent. Share them; your competition won't be surprised.

To many people, creating a Be Different business strategy means building a strategy with a truly unique intent; one in which the fundamental direction chosen for the organization around its various elements — such as markets, products, pricing, differentiation, partnerships and alliances, and sales — is fundamentally different from that of all other competitors.

Second, it is highly questionable whether any organization can realistically claim their strategy is truly unique from all of its competitors. Finally, even if it were unique, the strategy would not, in and of itself, guarantee success.

All strategies are inherently flawed; none are perfect. Strategy builders cannot possibly have all the information they require in order to develop a flawless strategic direction. They must, nevertheless, make strategy decisions based on the best information available. That's just the way it is. Getting your strategy fundamentally right is a vital ingredient to success. However, there are other elements of strategy building that provide tremendous opportunities for improving your chances of success.

The reality is that the strategy document for many businesses could be shared with their competitors and most of them would not be very surprised.

There is generally a limit to the options available to most organizations in terms of the alternatives and potential directions for them to take. In addition, most organizations tend to choose generically similar strategies such as competing on customer service, new product innovation, price and best value. This often occurs as the result of applying the benchmarking process; choosing options that work for the best-in-class organizations rather than breaking out of the box to create a truly innovative approach to win in the market.

So, if it's not the essence of strategy that positions an organization to survive the vagaries of market forces, what will enable it to Be Different and be successful? It starts with simplifying the process of creating your strategy. If your strategy is flawed due to incomplete information, changing market conditions and limitations on the strategic choices available to you, why not have a strategic development process that enables you to find your direction fast? Then you can move on to the most effective things you can do for the success of your strategy. Let's begin by exploring the notion of simplifying the strategy development process, moving on to some other ways to enhance its success in the marketplace.

Chapter Eight

Having been an active participant in strategy building sessions for over thirty years, I have developed the anatomy of a strategic planning retreat that describes what goes on in one of these sessions when executives grapple with the challenge of building a strategy for their organization.

- Strategy building teams are sequestered off-site to examine, without daily distractions, the future needs of the organization.

- Numerous subject matter experts (SMEs) are introduced to make presentations on the key issues facing the business, including the competition, the economy, financial outlook, technological change and other related topics. Be prepared for the SMEs to strut their stuff, provide far too much detail and overly complicate strategy building efforts.

- Rigorous and complicated analysis, backed up by charts, graphs and research by experts, is given to each of the key issues facing the business. Information overload would be an understatement. Drinking through a fire hose would aptly describe the process. Handouts are provided to show the participants that the work done is thorough and trustworthy.

- Break-out sessions are held to assess critical challenges and to brainstorm solutions.

- Detailed minutes of the session are prepared, summarizing the issues discussed and the direction that has been agreed upon.

- Comments from all participants are requested back to the strategic planning coordinator within a few weeks.

- These comments are distilled by the strategic planning folks and fed back to the session participants.

- At some point a decision is actually made on the fundamental direction the organization must take in order to meet the challenges that have been identified.

- Then, the agreed-upon direction is farmed out to strategy primes who are asked to prepare specific objectives with action plans to begin the strategy implementation process.

Your strategy must result in action, so keep it simple, get to the gut issues quickly and act.

With such an elaborate process, it's easy to lose sight of the end game. At times I have concluded that we have created a platform for the experts in the organization to impress us. Indeed, I have participated in some of these strategy building sessions where the criteria for success seemed to be how complicated you could make the content and the process.

I have always had difficulty with this approach because I have seen a Be Different approach work much more effectively. It is based on the notion of dumbing it down: that simple is good but simpler is better. Sooner or later your strategy must result in action, so it makes sense to keep it simple, get to the gut issues quickly and make the key decisions that will have a dramatic impact on the performance of your organization.

The Be Different strategic planning model that has been successful for me involves essentially four components:

- Creating your Strategic Game Plan

- Developing your Execution and Accountability Plan

- Employing a Team Workshop Process

- Reviewing your progress regularly

Answer three questions and you have your strategy.

Typically your Strategic Game Plan is developed by answering three fundamental questions. Thanks to my friend and colleague Rick Knowlan of Knowlan Consulting in Vancouver (www.knowlan.com), who introduced me to this approach while I was leading businesses within BC Telecom.

The questions are:

1. HOW BIG do you want to be?

2. WHO do you want to SERVE?

3. HOW will you compete and WIN?

■ The number of strategic alternatives facing most organizations is limited; the essence of most strategies wouldn't really surprise most of their competitors. Since this is the case, why not adopt a Be Different strategy building process that quickly determines your general strategic direction and simplifies the details necessary to see it implemented?

■ Try the four step process to create your strategic game plan in a team setting with a detailed action plan to implement the steps to see your game plan come to life.

■ The *Be simple* approach to creating a strategic game plan for an organization involves answering three questions that deal with the essence of any good strategy:

1. What are your financial goals in order to satisfy the owners of the business?

2. Who are the customers to whom you intend allocating scarce resources because you believe they represent the best economic opportunity for the firm?

3. How do you intend to compete with the other companies available to your targeted customers and win?

■ A game plan crafted with tender loving care around these questions will put your organization in a Be Different class by itself.

Chapter Nine

HOW BIG Do You Want to Be?

HOW BIG is a question about your financial growth aspirations. The answer should drive strategy development but very often it is the last thing that is considered. In most strategy building exercises, the strategy is created first and then the financial results of the strategy are determined. The finance staff and the CEO review the financial strategy and guess what they say? The strategy is not good enough because the financial results are unacceptable.

Sound familiar? This is then communicated back to the strategy team which is directed to strengthen the financial targets and resubmit them for approval. This process is repeated and continues until the executive accept the financial aims. I have seen it take weeks and sometimes months to finally complete.

Financial goals determine the character of your strategy.

If the nature of the game is to build the strategy and then jockey back and forth until acceptable financial goals are produced, the overall strategic process becomes overly complicated as well as time and resource consuming. To those who are constantly complaining that the strategic development process needs to be simplified, I suggest that what is needed is to first set the financial targets and then build the strategy to deliver them.

The benefits of this approach at the strategy setting level flow through to developing the departmental budgets that will provide resources to achieve the strategy. Departments are given the high level targets that satisfy the strategic financial goals. It is then up to each department to work out the details for implementing the tactics and programs and obtain the resources to make them happen. How simple is that? Funny that most department heads don't like overall budget targets handed to them even in the spirit of simplification.

Incremental financial objectives produce minimal-change strategies with low risk. Bold financial results come from more aggressive riskier ones.

Incremental financial objectives produce minimal change strategies with low attendant risk. If, on the other hand, bolder financial results are expected, you need to pursue a more aggressive and riskier strategy. You can't have an incremental strategy and expect bold financial improvement.

But many leaders do. I am not talking about the situation where there is a debate over the assumptions behind the numbers, for indeed the assumptions need to be the most realistic possible and must be acceptable to all. Rather, I am referring to the situation where, even though everyone is in agreement with the drivers of the strategy, the leaders of the organization want better numbers from it. This approach is extremely dangerous as it unhooks the inherent cause and effect relationship between strategy and financial results.

Furthermore, the insistence on having better numbers without changing the underlying strategy can cause internal problems. People like to feel that the strategic goals are realistic and achievable; when bigger numbers are squeezed out of a strategy and there is no debate about the drivers of that strategy, motivation suffers and people give up.

Be Different companies are tenacious in morphing from a strategy-drives-financials paradigm to the financials-drive-strategy one. They recognize that this approach simplifies the strategy building and its consequent budgeting process while accelerating the process of choosing a direction and then moving to execute the plan.

So, what could the answers to the HOW BIG question look like? It all depends on the specific challenges being faced by a particular organization. Here are some examples:

- We will grow top line revenue by 20% each year for the next three years.

- We will increase earnings before interest, taxes, depreciation and amortization (EBITDA) by 5% by 2010.

- We will generate ten million dollars in sales from new products over the next thirty-six months while maintaining gross margins at 30%.

- We will maintain the current sales growth rate of 15% per annum for the next twenty-four months.

Be Different companies morph from a strategy-drives-financials paradigm to a financials-drive-strategy one.

I recently assisted a local company, ARA Safety, in reviewing their existing strategy. I was impressed when James Fierro, the chairman, got up in front of his management team and told them that their target was to achieve a share price of $X and in order to get there, they had to generate $Y in sales revenue at assumed multiple of Z-times. He then stated that the purpose of the session was to review the existing strategy along with the plans and programs necessary to deliver these financial objectives. There was to be no debate over the market and financial targets. They were a given. They must be respected. Their role was to achieve them.

An excellent example of strong, effective leadership coupled with clearly stated expectations.

■ The character of your strategy depends on how bold your financial goals are. Start the process with a debate. A strategy with aggressive annual targets will require higher risk and choices that will be completely different than in a strategy built to achieve modest financial goals.

■ Don't try to squeeze better numbers out of a given strategy. Change the strategy to achieve a higher level of performance.

Chapter Ten

WHO Do You Want to SERVE?

Not every customer is a good customer. Not all customers are created equal. There is no such thing as a bad customer; it's just that some are better than others. You've heard the expressions. The point is that each customer represents a different economic opportunity for an organization. Some have a higher profit potential than others. So, it is extremely important that you carefully choose the customers that you want to attract.

There is no such thing as a bad customer; it's just that some are better than others.

Rarely does an organization have an infinite number of resources to address and serve every group of customers — to be all things to all people. So this question is all about choice. On which customer segments should you concentrate your efforts? Where do you want the resources of your organization to be deployed? This is an extremely critical aspect of strategy development and many factors must be considered in making the right choice.

Here are some questions an organization should ask itself in reaching a decision:

• What customer segments do we now serve?

- What are the growth rates of each? What are the fastest growing segments?

- What are the top three segments in terms of growth?

- Which segments are aligned with the organization's core competencies?

- Is geography a good way to look at customer segmentation?

- Which segments are easy to access with minimal cost?

- Are there currently any unserviced segments that we could enter?

- What is the competition in the various segments?

- Which segments yield the highest value in the long run?

- Are there regulatory or government policy hurdles that we would have to overcome to serve specific segments?

- What are the current barriers to competitive entry?

- Where do we have significant *barriers to customer exit*?

Lifetime value = present value + strategic value. It separates the good customers from the great ones.

The *lifetime value* of a customer is the most meaningful way to look at the financial benefits a customer brings to an organization.

Here is the equation:

Lifetime Value = Present Value + Strategic Value

Where:

Present value is the value of customers based on what they currently spend with you;

Strategic value is the value of customers based on their potential spending with you over some future period.

This assumes that you can grow the customer in terms of the amount of business they do with you today. Sources of growth would include increasing your share of wallet with the customer, selling additional products and services and charging higher prices to reflect planned added value to them.

Think about it another way:

Strategic Value = Current Spending + Future Spending

Of course as you look to grow customers, don't forget that you need to protect their current spending; if customers dump your current products and services you will have a much larger problem.

Note that value can be measured in whatever manner is meaningful and appropriate to your organization. Some companies measure revenue; others are able to calculate profit on a customer basis and use that as the metric. Once you have evaluated the lifetime value of the customer segments you are considering, prioritize them in order to understand which segment your organization should target.

The choice you make about WHO to SERVE must be consistent with your financial goals (the answer to the HOW BIG question). The financial targets of your organization should inform and guide every aspect of its strategy. The strategy is being built to deliver the stated financial goals. It is futile to choose a customer group to serve that is consistent with your core competencies but whose growth rate will not deliver the economic results expected.

If a customer segment can't deliver your financial goals why would you bother with it?

Targeting a customer segment that has a sales growth potential of 5%, for example, makes little sense if the financial objective is to grow top line revenues by 15% per year. You must choose a customer target that has the potential to generate the financial returns expected.

Once your organization has decided who to target, you need to decide on which customers to walk away from — who to dump. Most businesses don't have sufficient resources to take on new customers and continue to serve the existing ones. You need to walk away from those customer segments that cannot deliver your financial goals. This is tough for most organizations to do, but it is critical to successful strategy deployment.

Once you decide who to serve, you need to decide who to dump.

QUICK HITS

- You need to choose customers who will satisfy your established financial goals; a low growth customer segment is not good enough if you have high growth financial expectations.

- Consider the Lifetime Value (LTV) of a customer as a way of making the choice of who to serve; LTV = Present Value + Strategic Value over the time a customer is expected to be with you.

- Dump the customers that you choose not to serve, even though it is a painful process.

Chapter Eleven

HOW Will You Compete and WIN?

Let's review our strategic game plan work so far. We have set the financial goals for the business over, say, the next thirty-six months and we have chosen the customer segments that will be our engine to deliver our desired economic results. The next step is to determine how we intend to compete and win in the target customer segments. This is, without a doubt, the most critical part of the strategy work. It is the part where you declare how you intend to Be Different from your competitors and beat them handily.

The most critical part of your strategy is how you intend to Be Different from your competitors and beat them in the trenches.

In Section One, we discussed the ultimate manifestation of Being Different: the ability to articulate clearly your competitive value differences and compose your organization's *only* statement. It is now time to return to this work and use it to answer the HOW to WIN question. Here are some of the issues that should be considered:

- What are the top priority customer needs and expectations of the chosen customer segments?

- Who are the principal competitors in each segment? How do

they compete? How do they intend to win? How successful are they?

- What are their strengths and weaknesses?

- What value differences does your organization currently have that could be leveraged against your competition?

- What added-value differences would place your business beyond the competition? What would it take to develop them and flawlessly execute them in the market?

- Are there different ways, compared to the competition, you could meet the critical expectations of your customers?

Organizations answer the HOW to WIN question in a multitude of ways. In terms of the *only* statement examples used in Section One, here are a couple of hypothetical HOW to WIN statements.

'We will compete and win by:

'Providing personal development coaching for MBA students to build their individual strengths as well as specialized electives tailored to the specific career aspirations of each. This will all be done within a student team context to enable students to build their leadership and interpersonal skills to prepare them for the organizational environment.'(for Queen's School of Business)

'Providing personalized Internet search engine capabilities that enhance the value of social interaction and networking.' (for Whrrl)

A financial services business I once worked with developed this HOW to WIN strategy:

'We will compete and win by:

- Leveraging the intimate understanding we have of the customer

- Providing personalized holistic financial-based solutions

- Matching our advisors specifically with each customer

- Delivering knock your socks off customer service'

A great effort. Even though more precision is required to be more specific on each strategy element, its competitive positioning essentially involves using customer relationship management techniques to learn as much as it can about each customer and using this information to create personalized solutions for each one. From an operational perspective, the company intends to assign financial advisors to members based on their specific characteristics and provide superlative customer service to them.

As the former Senior VP Marketing of BC Telecom, I devised the following HOW to WIN statement:

'Our basic competitive approach will be to develop intimate one-to-one relationships with our customers and create our offers to match each one's unique needs and preferences.'

The answer to the HOW to WIN question not only has profound implications for overall strategic capability development for an organization, it also has an immediate operational benefit for those frontliners who are constantly dealing with customers or potential customers. They must be able to answer the question 'Why should I do business with you as opposed to XYZ Company?' If they can't answer this question, your frontliners are helplessly stranded in never-never land. The HOW to WIN answer gives them ammunition to effectively answer this question and hopefully increase the rate of customer acquisition.

If frontline people can't answer the customer question 'Why should I do business with you as opposed to someone else?' you haven't done your only work.

A credit union client I worked with discovered during a mystery shopping exercise they were conducting in a number of their branches that their financial reps simply could not answer the question 'Why should I do business with you as opposed to the banks?' They were surprised by the question and were very uncomfortable in trying to answer it, resorting to a general response that credit union members are owners of the company (not a unique attribute). Not at all what the right answer should be. And not an answer that will help you acquire customers. This was clearly not the rep's fault; the credit union had not developed a crisp clean HOW to WIN strategy statement.

QUICK HITS

■ HOW to WIN is the most critical aspect of your strategy building as it puts words in your frontliners' mouths about why someone should do business with you instead of with your competition. Here is a step-by-step approach to determine HOW to WIN:

1. Select the customer needs and expectations you intend to satisfy from the segment you have chosen to serve.

2. Examine the internal opportunities to Be Different outlined in Section One.

3. Evaluate exactly where the competition is focusing their efforts: Which segments? Their selling proposition? Market success? Vulnerabilities?

4. Decide on what basis you intend to compete, win and create a unique value proposition, i.e. what unique value benefits do you promise your chosen customers?

5. Create your *only* statement.

6. Use the *only* statement to develop your HOW to WIN positioning statement.

Chapter Twelve

The Strategic Game Plan Statement

HOW BIG do you want to be? WHO do you want to SERVE? HOW will you WIN? Once the answer to each of these questions is clear, the *Strategic Game Plan* needs to be created.

The Strategic Game Plan statement represents the essence of your strategy. It not only directs new activity and behaviors in the organization, it also acts as the main communications vehicle to your employees to describe your future strategic direction.

The Strategic Game Plan statement is your strategic anchor; it communicates the essence of your strategy.

It is developed from the answers to the three questions discussed above, and it looks like this:

> 'We intend to (HOW BIG) by [desired time frame] by focusing our scarce resources on (WHO to SERVE). We will compete and win by (HOW to WIN).'

Here is an example of the Strategic Game Plan Statement that was created by the financial services client I mentioned earlier who was interested in building its capabilities in serving the high net worth customer segment.

'We intend to grow revenue from the Mass Affluent / Emerging Wealthy market segments from $X Million in 2005 to $Y Million by the end of 2010. We will focus our resources on the Mass Affluent sub-segments of Commuter Homesteads, Urban Gentry and Cruising Commuters of community Z with a view to expand into Greater Vancouver in February 2008.

We will compete and WIN by

- Leveraging the intimate understanding we have of the customer

- Providing personalized holistic financial based solutions

- Matching our Advisors specifically with each customer, and

- Delivering knock your socks off customer service'

One other hypothetical example to underscore this important idea:

'We will grow our top line revenues by 30% per year for the next 36 months by focusing our scarce resources on the male seniors' market in the Vancouver Lower Mainland. We will compete and win by providing personalized vacation service packages that leverage our CRM capabilities and external business relationships.'

Imagine the action that is possible with such a game plan statement! Is it clear? Do you think employees would get it? Does it direct the resources of the firm? Does it drive a stake in the Be Different competitive ground? Absolutely! This is how to develop strategy. This is how to capture the hearts and minds of the people you need to carry out your game plan and make you successful.

QUICK HITS

■ The Strategic Game Plan Statement combines the answers to the questions: HOW BIG? WHO to SERVE? HOW to WIN?

■ Your Strategic Game Plan Statement not only provides succinct strategic direction for your organization, it also provides an excellent communications vehicle for the rest of your organization. So use it.

Chapter Thirteen

Dumb It Down: The Execution and Accountability Plan

Of course, the strategic game plan alone doesn't ensure your success. You need to go to the next step and develop your execution and accountability plan which addresses how you will bring the game plan to life. It answers these three questions:

- What are the key things that need to be done to deliver the strategic game plan?

- When do they need to be done?

- Who will be held accountable for getting them done?

If people are not accountable, nothing happens.

To provide structure to this process, I often ask these questions of the major departments that are the main stakeholders in an organization and responsible for the successful execution of any strategy. These include marketing, sales, service, human resources, finance, operations, information technology and business development. Furthermore, all departments must review and eliminate non-strategic activities.

The following is intended to be a guide for objectives that could be set within each functional area. I have chosen the objectives that tend to have the major influence on the strategic game plan outcome.

- In Marketing – revenue by product and by market segment, market share, customer share, pricing, sales channels, customer communications, new product introduction, product rationalization and new skills and competencies such as database marketing, discussed later in the marketing section

- In Sales – revenue by product and by sales channel, sales differentiation strategy, training, customer account planning, consultative selling, and new skills and competencies

- In Service – service strategy, customer satisfaction measurements / targets, loyalty building initiatives and internal quality measurement

- In Human Resources – organizational structure to deliver on the strategic game plan, reward and recognition systems, position competencies and accountabilities, recruitment and retention tactics, employee performance and development plans

- In Finance – financial statements for key organizational elements driving the strategic game plan and margins

- In Operations – product fulfillment capabilities, process re-engineering and measurement, performance metrics/targets, service strategy delivery

- In Information Technology – CRM capability development, tracking key performance metrics

- In Business Development – alliances and partnerships, acquisitions and business integration competencies

- In Non-strategic Activity – define non-strategic activities with resources consumed. Define plans to release, reallocate and terminate resources; make budget adjustments

A word of warning: There is an overwhelming temptation at this stage to come up with as many objectives as you can think of that are related to getting the strategic game plan implemented. In fact it can turn into a brainstorming session which tends to be more about volume of activity than effectiveness. It is critical that objectives be carefully evaluated and prioritized in terms of their relative impact on delivering the game plan.

Consider this process of reviewing your objectives to boil them down to the critical few:

1. Define objectives for each functional area as discussed above.

2. Prioritize the list using impact on delivering the strategic game plan criteria.

3. Select the 20% that will likely deliver 80% of the results. Start with eliminating the least important and work up to the most important. Keep the process going until you are satisfied that you have the minimum number of objectives that will deliver the maximum of your game plan.

Too many objectives paralyzes progress; define the critical few and do them.

There is one last thing to consider in doing your execution and accountability work. Every strategy I ever developed carried with it the need to assign someone senior in the organization to oversee the implementation activities. I created what I called the *strategy hawk* for this purpose and usually assumed the role myself, delegating the detailed monitoring and follow-up work to one of my closest and most trusted executives reporting directly to me.

This person had a great deal of currency in the organization, and was proficient at staying on top of things and tenacious in prodding people along to fulfill their commitments. The strategy building team knew that we would be closely monitoring how effectively the agreed-upon objectives were being achieved. Creating this role had a profound effect on people's attitude toward game plan implementation.

Giving this role to someone reporting directly to me, and the fact that I would be getting regular reports on progress, issues and roadblocks, communicated the importance of the task and that it would not go away. There would be follow-up and key people would be held accountable.

Strategy hawk nirvana is to have the CEO assume the role. Who better than the CEO to hold people accountable and keep the strategy in the faces of the leadership team? Who better to direct corrective action when things aren't going as planned?

As a rule, CEOs don't take on the role; they ask their strategic planners to do it. Darren Entwistle, TELUS CEO, is an exception. In TELUS there is no question of who owns the strategy and its execution.

Every organization needs a strategy hawk to drive implementation.

Darren is tenacious about assigning people who report directly to him and others in the organization to the critical tasks that must be achieved to deliver the company's strategy. And he is relentless in holding people accountable. Darren maintains this strategy by holding regular *strat-check* sessions to review the implementation progress. These are intense affairs that drill down on every aspect of the organization's strategy, critically examining any deviation from plan and detailing any corrective action to be taken.

■ The game plan statement without a navigational chart to execute it is a pipe dream.

■ To successfully execute your strategy you need detailed objectives and action plans, with people held accountable to complete them.

■ Don't create too many objectives as you develop your game plan. Refine objectives to a critical few that will have a maximum impact on your strategy implementation.

■ Assign a *strategy hawk* to be the eyes and ears watching over the execution of the objectives and action plans that have been committed to. Pick the most detail-oriented, persistent and tenacious person for the role. The strategy hawk will delight your team with the progress you achieve.

■ If you can get the CEO to be the strategy hawk, all the better.

Chapter Fourteen

Most strategy development involves consultants coming into an organization and performing a detailed assessment and analysis of the factors that should guide the development of the strategy. This process is often quite lengthy and complex and it can consume significant time and resources of the client organization. I am not condemning this approach as it does yield results for which organizations are willing to pay substantial amounts of money.

In the spirit of *Be Simple*, however, I suggest that there is an approach that has several advantages over the traditional consulting method. This is to employ a team workshop process. It is a straightforward approach and not particularly revolutionary. But it works. Design the workshop to involve those people critical to the success of the strategy. The number of people involved in the workshop is usually not an issue, although I prefer a group in the range of eight to ten. Use the team to create the strategic game plan.

The advantages of the workshop approach over the traditional consulting engagement process are:

- Lower investment from your organization in terms of consulting fees. In many situations, you might be looking at a fee difference between hundreds of thousands of dollars and tens of thousands of dollars.

- Information generated is only that needed to make the specific tough decisions on strategy. I have been frustrated in the past with consultants who would produce volumes and volumes of data and analysis which were never used in the formulation of our strategy but did enhance the amount of fees paid.

Be Simple; use the expertise of a team to create your strategy.

- Substantially less time is consumed. Typically, a strategy with detailed objectives can be built over a three to four day period.

- Participants own the strategy and its results, the consultant doesn't. Expertise comes from those people in the organization accountable to lead it. This results in more buy-in and commitment to the chosen course of action.

- Teamwork is strengthened by people who are critical to the successful execution of the strategy. Members of the strategy building team must work together to create the strategy, and they all have to agree with it before it is finalized.

- The focus is on strategy execution, the often forgotten part of strategic planning.

QUICK HITS

■ The most effective overall process to develop your Strategic Game Plan is to gather the strategy stakeholders in a room for three to four days and work hard to complete it.

■ The workshop players need to be the individuals who are accountable for the strategy's success and have a vested interest in seeing it succeed.

■ Workshops are great for teambuilding and afford the opportunity to build a stronger bond among the participants.

■ Build your strategy in three days; execute it on the fourth.

Chapter Fifteen

Dumb It Down: The Progress Review

The last component to dumb down your strategic planning process involves a periodic review of the progress being made to execute it in the market. The process is to assemble the strategy workshop team chaired by the strategy hawk every quarter and go through each objective and action plan to determine whether or not it is on track. Where the chosen strategic direction represents a significant departure from past practice, you might decide to meet more frequently, say monthly, to have a closer look at how the implementation is proceeding.

The strategy hawk reviews progress every three months and takes action to deal with execution shortfalls.

The output from a progress review session is an action plan addressing those objectives that are falling behind, with individuals assigned certain tasks to get things back on track by a specific date. This action plan portfolio then forms a part of the agenda for the next progress review. This structured approach is very effective in keeping the implementation of your strategic game plan alive.

■ Schedule regular reviews of your strategy. If your new direction is significantly different from the past, schedule reviews more frequently.

■ Regularly communicate your progress throughout the organization.

■ Use your strategy hawk to organize and lead the sessions.

Chapter Sixteen

Focus. Focus. Focus.

Going hand in hand with dumbing down the strategy process is the need to focus your efforts on the few things that matter, alluded to earlier in the need to concentrate on a small number of objectives, for example. That would deliver the highest percentage of results — a stark contrast for those of us who, in the past, have been involved in strategy building sessions that resulted in more objectives and action plans than could ever be implemented. The reality was that we were trying to do more than existing levels of resources would allow.

Unfortunately, this is a common dilemma. Many strategy sessions outline a multitude of objectives and action plans that are simply unrealistic. In addition, there is no prioritizing. It is a brainstorming dump or a wish list of things that could be done, with little understanding of the strategic priority of the objectives or the ability to deliver given resource realities.

Roy's Rule of Three: Find the three things that will achieve 80% of your strategy and do them.

The truth is there is a limit to what an organization can deliver at one time; it is a function of what people are currently doing and the attendant bandwidth available to take on anything new. In strategy development you need to cut through this gridlock if you want to see new things done.

The test question: If you have people, time and money to do only three things, what would they be?

Roy's Rule of Three states that you need to find three things that will contribute to 80% of your success in executing your new strategy and do them. The exercise is not necessarily to choose three things, but rather the process in determining the small number of things that will deliver most of your strategy. It is a discipline that you need to follow after enumerating all your objectives and action plans.

Evaluate each from the point of strategy impact and devote resources to as few as you can. You may not get down to three but you will reduce the number of activities you need to fund in order of importance. It might not be three but it is unlikely to be twenty. The discipline of review is the important point.

Multi-tasking can be deadly in strategy execution.

Test your managers on this. If someone walks into your office and proudly tells you they are working on twelve key strategic initiatives, show them out of your office and ask them to return with justification that twelve things are mandatory in order to deliver 80% of the strategy, or to come back with three or four things that are.

I am not saying that an organization shouldn't be aware of and open to the possibilities available to them. The opponents of focus would say that to be unaware would mean opportunities lost as an organization moves forward. What I am saying is yes, be open to what is going on around you but choose to act on a few critical things when a decision is made on a specific course of action.

Remember, multi-tasking can be deadly in terms of implementing a strategy, and if you can't implement, you don't have a chance to Be Different.

- If you are not focused, you are wasting precious time and money.

- Pick the top three things that matter and do an exceptional job on them.

- Strategy is all about determining your future direction and then allocating resources to the few steps that will get you there.

Chapter Seventeen

Cut the Crap

Strategy sessions always seem to concentrate on the new things that you need to do to build the business. They rarely spend the time required to determine the things that you should stop doing. In other words, the activities that are associated with the old strategy and that are no longer consistent with the new direction of the organization rarely get any strategic attention.

You can't create a new strategy today and yet continue to do the same things you were doing yesterday. You do not have the resources or bandwidth to both keep the past alive and determine your new future at the same time, yet many organizations do not allocate the resources necessary to eliminate non-strategic elements.

Strategy building is just as much about not doing, as it is about doing. Therefore, assign an executive to show the rest of the organization that it is important to eliminate the things that are holding the organization back. Develop an inventory of *crap* along with the expenses currently being incurred by that crap. Then reallocate the resources and expenses to strategic activities and stop the naysayers who preach that there are no resources available to implement the new strategy.

Here are some typical candidates for crap that you should be alert for:

- Customers who are not able to generate sufficient revenue or profit directed by the HOW BIG strategic question

- Products and services no longer consistent with your future direction

- Training programs that are out of date

- Advertising programs supporting the old direction

- Business development activities pursuing opportunities no longer on strategy

- Technology development programs

- Operational improvement activities supporting the old direction but no longer of value

---

Your new strategy demands you let go of non-strategic work; assign a cut the crap champion.

In addition, when you have identified non-strategic activities to be discontinued in order to free up the space necessary to do the critical right things, make sure that at the same time you remove their associated expenses from the departmental budgets of those who are currently engaged in them. If this is not done, people will continue to spend the money and you will never see it, effectively making it impossible to reallocate it to the new strategic plan.

If the marketing department with a budget of one million dollars, for example, is currently developing a product that is no longer needed, stop the activity, remove the money from its budget and give it to another department that needs it to advance the new strategy.

Also, beware of people in your organization who are guardians of the past, or *irrelevance managers*. These are individuals who like doing what they have always done, who resist and deny the need to change and will subvert all attempts to change the direction of the organization now on a different path.

In order to address this, a cut-the-crap executive champion needs to be assigned to lead the charge to cleanse the internal environment, to identify individuals currently engaged in non-strategic activities and to convince them to take on work associated with the new strategic direction. If they can't, then these individuals need to be removed from the organization with dignity. If not, they will infect those who are truly excited about change and will impede the progress toward your new goals.

Irrelevance managers need to go with the crap they produce.

QUICK HITS

■ Just as you need to walk away from customers who are not in your strategic sights, you need to discontinue all projects and related activities that are not providing value in terms of your new strategy.

■ Let a cut-the-crap champion loose to get the job done.

■ Beware of the *custodians of irrelevance* who linger throughout your organization trying desperately to hang on to the things that were required of them in the past but are no longer necessary.

■ Take them aside and give them new assignments in line with your new directions; if they are not willing to go in the new direction get rid of them.

■ Irrelevance managers will infect the organization. If you don't deal with them, they will infect others to maintain the status quo.

Chapter Eighteen

Be Anal about Execution

Management guru Peter Drucker referred to plans as 'only good intentions unless they immediately degenerate into hard work.' He also said, being much focused on the importance of execution, that the biggest challenge for most businesses is executing well — not devising 'helium-filled plans' for reaching the next level.

Here's the model for my thinking in this area.

- Doing something is ten times better than talking about it. Unless someone actually does something the cognitive process alone is of limited value.

- The perfect plan that can't be executed is worthless.

- The *just about right* plan with flawless execution yields brilliant results. This is the modus operandi of the Be Different business strategy which informs the direction to take. Execution drives the results.

The principle should be: get your strategy just about right and execute it flawlessly. Former President D. D. Eisenhower is reputed to have said a good plan violently executed now, is better than a perfect plan next week. This means spending the appropriate amount of time on the details of the action plan with individual accountability and time frames for their completion. It means looking at every action plan in its relation to every other one to ensure they all consume time in a manner that is consistent with established priorities.

Darren Entwistle assumed the strategy hawk role and personally leads the execution of the TELUS strategy. He is expert in defining the essence of what is required to make the company successful and then moving on and making it happen. TELUS' acquisition of Clearnet, the wireless company based in Toronto, is a case in point. Prior to his arrival at TELUS, acquiring a national wireless capability was a strategic priority for the company but it was not given a green light to proceed. Darren arrived, quickly confirmed that the strategy made sense, sold the Board on the idea and did the deal in a matter of months despite all the issues and concerns that were raised along the way. A good example of being focused and relentless about execution? Absolutely.

The just-about-right strategy with flawless execution yields brilliant results.

QUICK HITS

- The essence of a Be Different strategy is one that gets the direction just about right and executes it with absolute precision.

- Winners execute plans better than losers.

- A great strategy that can't be executed is worthless.

- A good strategy that can be executed is great.

- Some say planning is unproductive; put your 'execution lenses' on and make planning productive.

Chapter Nineteen

Plan on the Run

The five year strategic plan is the antithesis of *planning on the run.*

Does a five year plan actually achieve what is intended? What would you say the overall percentage success rate of a five year plan is? Do you think it is higher than 50%? How about in year five? Optimistically, you can expect a success rate of 25%. Does the plan actually deliver what you have planned for in that year? Not likely.

The five year strategic plan is the antithesis of planning on the run.

At best, the time frame of this type of plan provides direction only, a reference point from which to deviate as you carry your strategic plan forward. I suggest you start out with a thirty-six month plan and do your best to determine your operating environment to that time. This will be difficult to do for the same reasons as a five year plan, but the time horizon is at least more reasonable and manageable.

There is a reason I talk about a thirty-six month rather than a three year plan. You need to try to compress in whatever way you can the planning time horizon so you keep *execution* as a key driver of your work. To someone in a team helping to create strategy, it is far more action-oriented to consider what you need to do thirty-six months out versus three years from now.

Some say a horizon longer than three years is necessary to get people to commit to radical change in an organization's strategy, that with a period shorter than five years people have a hard time imagining revolutionary change, even if that is what is required to make an organization successful. I don't see it that way. The strategic game plan statement discussed earlier will capture the essence of what the organization must achieve over an indefinite time horizon; what is relevant and essential to realizing this future desired state is a concrete action plan dealing with the essentials of implementation. Otherwise nothing happens and no progress is made.

Choose a thirty-six month plan rather than a three year plan; compress the time horizon to keep execution as the activity driver.

In addition to having a short term strategy horizon, you also need to think of your plan as a living organism. This metaphor is intended to get you thinking about keeping your strategy *alive.* Always be constantly in touch with it and look for aspects no longer valid so you can take appropriate action.

There are two uses of a strategy document:

- The traditional, more common view is that a strategic planning document communicates the essence of the planned future direction of an organization.

- I agree with this, but suggest that it doesn't go far enough to capture the *planning on the run* dimension; for this we need to define the strategy planning document as a repository of lessons learned as well. In other words, once the direction for the organization has been decided on and articulated, the experiences encountered during its execution in the real world need to be recorded so that learning can occur and the direction can be adjusted accordingly. Use the strategy document for this.

To see if you are treating your strategy document as a living one, where what you learn is captured and analyzed, simply look at it. Does it have coffee stains on it? Are the edges of some pages bent over? Does it have handwritten comments in red ink on it? Are there additional sheets of paper attached to it with empirical results and associated evaluation? Is it rather crumpled or does it look like you have just finished ironing it?

Your strategy document is a repository of learnings. Write on it! Mess it up!

If it looks like the day you or your consultant developed it, then it is likely that you have done nothing with it. The more rough and rugged the document looks, the more it has been used and the more likely that you have actually achieved some of its results. Mess it up. Spill stuff on it. Rip the pages. Abuse it!

Your strategy needs to be constantly in touch with both execution effectiveness and market dynamics in order to test its relevance. Here is my simple process to capture what needs to be done:

1. Plan
2. Execute
3. Learn

4. Adjust
5. Go back to execute

It is straightforward: create the strategy, start executing it, learn about the impacts it makes in the real world, adjust your strategy based on what you have learned and then quickly go back to execution.

QUICK HITS

- Think about your strategy document as a repository of learnings, a document intended to record successes and failures.

- If your strategy document isn't messed up, it hasn't been used; hence it has not provided guidance to make it more successful.

- If your strategy is not adjusted based on real world results, it is nothing more than a theory.

- Learn the plan-on-the-run process: plan, execute, learn, adjust and go back to execute.

Planning on the run = plan, execute, learn, adjust, execute.

Chapter Twenty

In this section I have presented a number of Be Different ideas to establish a more effective strategy building process for your organization. Let's now take a step back and integrate all the ideas into an overall strategic framework to see the interrelationships at play.

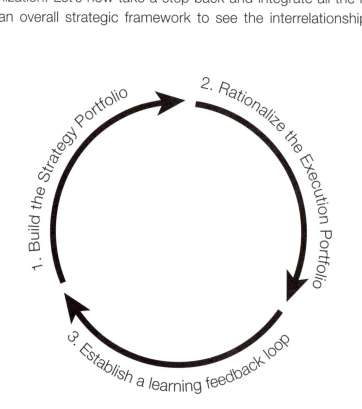

1. Build the Strategy Portfolio

2. Rationalize the Execution Portfolio

3. Establish a learning feedback loop

Let's explain:

1. Build the strategy portfolio. This step involves creating strategies at various levels in the organization. It starts with a strategy for the overall business which defines the context for all activity in the organization. It gives direction to every business unit; every department and all individuals specify the activities in which they should engage. How does the marketing department, for example, know what to do if it doesn't understand the basic strategic direction of the business? It doesn't. The problem is that if there is a strategic void at any organizational level, people will tend to do what they think is right. Well intended but a disaster in the works.

   And remember, each strategy should be simplified to quickly establish the essence of the direction to be taken. Each level of strategy informs the one below it: the overall business strategy informs each business unit strategy, each departmental strategy and all the way down to the performance plan for each person in the organization. This *strategic vertical integrity* is powerful in that it guarantees that all organizational units and people are aligned and acting synergistically.

Strategic vertical integrity guarantees that the organization is aligned to a common goal.

---

2. Rationalize the Implementation Portfolio. You need to have a portfolio of implementation programs that can deliver the strategic direction you have chosen. It should be designed with a minimum number of programs to deliver the maximum strategic results. Ideally, 20% of the execution effort should deliver 80% of your strategy. Work on this ratio until you are satisfied that you get this asymmetric result, and remember to cut the *crap* on activities that are related to past strategic directions but are irrelevant to the new plan.

3. Establish a learning feedback loop. Create a process to incorporate what you learn, from executing the strategy to planning on the run, into your ongoing strategy progress review. Adjust the strategy based on the real results achieved in the market. Communicate the adjustment of your strategy to the organization as an example of the organic nature of your plan, your nimbleness and flexibility to make the tough decisions, and your ability to adapt to what is being achieved in the trenches.

A learning feedback loop is necessary to plan on the run.

QUICK HITS

■ Strategy building for an organization involves ensuring that your overall business strategy drives all other lower level strategies at the departmental or business unit level. This is referred to as vertical integrity.

■ Once all of your strategies are aligned, make your implementation project portfolio as small as you can. Target to have the number of projects deliver 80+% of your strategy.

■ Create a process to ensure that implementation results are cycled back to the strategic portfolio to document the process, recording adjustments to the strategy plan.

✓ Create a strategic game plan for your business by addressing three critical questions:

- HOW BIG do you want to be?

- WHO do you want to SERVE?

- HOW are you going to compete and WIN?

✓ Develop detailed objectives and action plans that address how to implement the strategy.

✓ Prioritize the list of objectives to determine the critical few that will have the highest impact on strategy execution.

✓ Hold strategy owners accountable for their strategy deliverables.

✓ Assign a *strategy hawk* to lead the implementation process. You need a senior person to be in the faces of the people accountable for achieving the key objectives assigned to them.

✓ Use the workshop approach with the key owners of the strategy to develop it.

✓ Review the progress you are making on your strategy at least once a quarter.

✓ Focus. Focus. Focus. Determine the fewest number of things that will produce 80% of the strategy results and do them. Multi-tasking can be deadly.

✓ Cut the crap. Eliminate all activity that does not work toward implementing your new strategy and reassign the people associated with the non-strategic projects. You don't have the time or resources to do anything else. *Managers of irrelevance* must go as well.

✔ Be anal about execution. Ninety percent of winning is what you do in the trenches, not how pretty your plan is.

✔ Plan on the run. The success of your strategy will be determined by how well your organization listens to its successes and failures on a day to day basis. Use this experience to tweak your strategy on the go.

✔ Be Different organizations are informed by strategy and driven by execution. The basic elements of this process are:

- Build your strategic portfolio with vertical integrity. Start with a strategy for your overall organization and drive everything else from it.

- Set the ratio of your execution portfolio: 20% of the action to achieve 80% of the strategic results.

- Establish a learning feedback loop and modify your strategies on the results achieved.

Section Three

BE DiFFERENT Marketing — Customerize

3

Section Introduction

To Be Different, an organization needs to *customerize* its marketing strategy and its marketing culture. In many organizations today, marketing is not adequately customer focused to allow them to take the lead over their competitors. It is not that the Marketing 101 approach is wrong; it's just that it doesn't go far enough.

My view on this issue is considered controversial by many marketers who diligently invest in traditional marketing practices and who believe that the results of their efforts define their organization as truly customer focused. The issue for me is this: if you want to distinguish yourself, you need to Be Different in marketing and explore new paradigms that define what it means to live for the customer.

Customerization is a shift from developing products that satisfy broad markets to creating packaged offers for small customer groups.

So, what do I mean by *customerized* marketing? *Customerization* involves a fundamental shift in emphasis from developing products for broad market segments to creating packaged offers for small groups of customers. Market *customerization* involves moving from a pure product-oriented focus to a customer-oriented one in which both receive prominent status.

Chapter Twenty-One

Product Marketing

In the telecommunications business, telephone equipment manufacturers historically developed new product features they hoped the telephone companies would offer their customer base. To give you an idea of how they would take advantage of these new features, consider the simple example of caller ID that allows customers to see, via a display screen on their telephone set, the number of the person calling them. The marketing challenge was to first verify that there was a real demand for this product by employing standard methods like focus groups and market research surveys.

Having concluded that there was sufficient market demand to warrant the capital investment required, the subsequent steps involved pricing the product to derive certain margins and creating a customer communications strategy. The communication challenge was to brand the product, in this case as Calling Number Display, and to describe the customer benefits in the most compelling manner possible. These included being able to see who was calling and having control over incoming calls. The final step was to try to promote and sell this feature to as broad a market as possible in order to recover attendant costs and deliver a reasonable rate of return.

This example illustrates a common product marketing method: to promote technology capabilities to broad markets by highlighting their features and benefits for certain customers. The method is not unique to the telecommunications business. The home entertainment markets (DVDs, HD TVs, etc.) and personal device markets (iPods and mobile phones) are two other examples where the technological capabilities are promoted to customers. Most busi-nesses adopt this approach. Success is measured by the number of units sold. The more units sold the more successful the marketing effort; its primary intent is to acquire new customers for the product.

Adopt the technology, define the product and sell to as many customers as you can. That's the essence of product marketing.

Here are the steps usually followed in the product marketing process, illustrated by the figure below:

1. Select the product to sell based on the technological capabilities that are likely to be adopted by the market.

2. Determine the product feature you want to promote and the customer benefit you want to highlight.

3. Do a market analysis to determine the level of customer demand you could expect.

4. Sell the product to as many targeted customers in the market as you can.

The end objective is to get as many of the targeted customers as you can to buy the product, to maximize your share of the target market.

Adopt the technology, define the product and sell as much as you can. Again, the essence of product marketing.

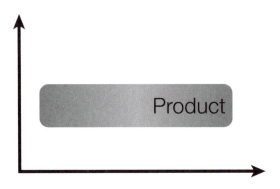

Chapter Twenty-Two

Customerized Marketing — BE DiFFERENT

Customerized marketing, on the other hand, involves adding a new dimension to the product marketing approach. In the customerized world, the primary focus is on creating packaged offers for small groups of customers.

The intent of customerized marketing is to:

- First, create new value for the customer as opposed to, in the product world, pushing an existing technological capability. Furthermore, the intent in customerized marketing is focused on building customer loyalty as well as on upselling new capabilities. You *create* in customerized marketing; you *push* in product marketing.

- Second, you want to customize the solution that you are trying to create. You want to make it as compelling and relevant to as small a group of customers as is practical. You want to be able to reflect the fact that each customer is unique, and therefore a more personalized approach is the most effective way to attract the customer's interest.

- Third, the focus for customerization is the building of an offer, not a product. As opposed to a product, an offer is very broad in the customer need set it is intended to satisfy. Creating an offer looks at the customer holistically and seeks to provide a packaged, multi-dimensional set of values driven by the many needs people have in their lives.

• Having created the packaged offer, the final step is to sell as many of them as possible to your small group of targeted customers.

Here are the steps usually followed in customerized marketing, illustrated by the figure below:

1. Choose the customer group that you want to target.

2. Analyze the customer group to determine their needs.

3. Create a number of relevant packaged offers that reflect this customer group's requirements.

4. Sell as many packaged offers as you can to the chosen customer group.

End objective – to get as much of the chosen customers' business as you can. Maximize your share of the customer's wallet.

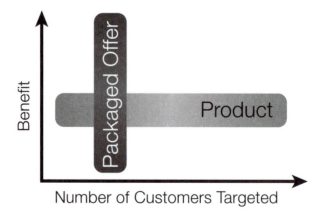

QUICK HITS

■ Let's look at both concepts side by side to clarify your understanding of each in order to implement Be Diffferent marketing in your organization.

Product Marketing	Customerized Marketing
Choose the product to sell	Choose the customer group to target
Select the benefit to promote	Analyze the customer group to target
Analyze the market	Create packaged offers
Sell the product to many customers	Sell multiple packaged offers to the selected customer groups
Acquire new customers	Build loyalty and upsell with chosen customer groups

Choose your high value customer group and penetrate it with as many packaged offers as you can. This is the customerized process.

Customerized marketing requires marketers to look at new ideas and adopt different ways of doing their jobs if they want to implement this new concept effectively. Let's examine them in the next chapters.

Chapter Twenty-Three

Customer Learning: Beyond Market Research

Customer learning is a giant leap beyond traditional market research. In order to understand this new concept, we need to understand the differences between the two. Let's begin by exploring the characteristics of market research.

Market Research

First, market research usually involves doing a periodic study of some sort. It can be a one-of-a-kind market analysis or it can be set up on a recurring basis.

The periodic nature of this traditional research approach, however, offers a mere snapshot of those customers at a specific chosen time, and therefore the results from the study will be influenced by the particular factors affecting them at that moment. If you only research a particular customer once or twice a year, it is difficult to get any continuity in that customer's wants, needs, expectations, behaviors, attitudes and views.

Next, the ability to extrapolate from this single snapshot data point and arrive at accurate long term conclusions about that customer's requirements is quite limited.

In addition, market research is usually done through an external company as most organizations don't have the internal expertise to do it, nor do they want to acquire the skills to make it a core competency of the organization. Moreover, they want the objectivity in the research results afforded by employing the services of an outside company.

As well, this traditional form of gathering customer information often takes a narrow view of the customer, exploring product categories like communications, mortgages, recreational property, etc. or attitudes on specific topics such as political preferences, government performance, health care improvements and so on.

Market research probes a few topics and doesn't yield a deep understanding of the customer.

Another factor in this type of customer research is that high level market segmentation defines the group of customers to study. As a rule, only a limited number of segmentation variables are used and they tend to be the common ones such as demographics and lifestyle preferences.

To those who may be unfamiliar with the term, a segmentation variable is a characteristic of the segment that you want to study. For example, a common segmentation variable that is used by most research is age; studies then gather information on people and categorize it by age group. Further, the segments derived from using a limited number of variables fall under common, easy-to-understand labels to describe them, such as:

- Male seniors in Greater Toronto

- Financial services

- Low income people

- The V4A 4A4 postal code in B.C.

- Chinese-Canadian families in Richmond B.C. with annual incomes over $100K

- Credit unions in Nova Scotia with revenues over two million dollars per annum

When you see these segment descriptors, it is relatively easy to get a picture of what the people in the segment look like. There is nothing wrong with this but the methodology has its limitations. By evaluating the population of customers in terms of only a few segmentation variables you end up with a few very large segments but knowing very little about each person in the segment other than the information provided by the segmentation variables used. It is assumed that the population mirrors the profile of a typical or average person in the segment on matters such as product and service preferences, political opinions and other topics of interest to the researchers.

For example, in the above figure, we could be looking at the 'V4A 4A4 postal code in B.C.' segment, and the only thing the people in the segment have in commom is their geographic location. They would no doubt have a variety of ethnic origins, earning levels, political ideologies, ideas about global warming, recreational preferences and attitudes on birth control. In addition, there would no doubt be a number of distinct sub-segments exhibiting common characteristics but different from the rest. In this case the *learning quotient*, the ability to gain insights about the customer from the segmentation data, would be very low, and the applications of the data very limited.

This type of segmentation may provide implications in terms of the attitudes, needs and expectations of each person in the segment, but definitive conclusions can't be made. Yet we do draw conclusions from data such as these. We develop a profile of the typical customer in a given market segment, we tend to buy products for this customer and we develop and communicate value propositions to people who exhibit the same characteristics as the segment overall.

We expect a high hit rate in sales and if the targeted customer actually looks like the profiled one in every respect — which is unlikely — we make a sale. But if by any chance the targeted customer is different from the profiled one — which is highly likely — we do not make a sale.

Market research has definite limitations but marketing people use it because it makes their lives easier.

If market research has these limitations, why is it used? Quite frankly, it makes life easier for the marketing folks. It is easier for marketing groups to approach a large segment of customers with a common sales pitch than it is to target different programs to many different customers with individualized sales pitches. But which one is more effective? Which one establishes a company as knowing the customer? Which one places the company in the Be Different class? It is the organization recognizing that every human being is unique. You too will discover this if you pay enough attention to detail and ask the right questions.

Finally, the last characteristic of market research that limits it as a Be Different approach is that everyone uses it. So how can you Be Different using a common practice? You can't. The good news is that you have an opportunity to adopt a new approach to gathering information about customers that will yield Be Different results for your organization: customer learning.

QUICK HITS

Market Research

- Conducted periodically.

- Conducted by an external firm.

- Looks at the customer from a narrow perspective: products and opinions.

- Uses a small number of variables to segment the market leading to a few large market segments defined but with little information about any single individual in the segment.

- Used by everyone. It can't Be Different.

Customer Learning

Here are the characteristics that differentiate customer learning from traditional market research.

First, as opposed to periodic studies, customer learning is a continuous process of probing customers. It is a process that fundamentally incorporates the fact that every customer is truly unique and that customers' needs, wants and expectations are never static. They change with the forces affecting the individual or the business and the environment in which they exist.

Second, customer learning engages the employees of the organization as opposed to the exclusive use of market research resources. An organization can learn much more about its customers if everyone from the frontline to the senior executive is involved in the process. In addition, it demonstrates that the organization wants to make knowledge about customers a core competency.

Customer learning takes a holistic view of the customer; avoids the narrow silo questions and asks the broader ones.

Third, rather than examining the narrow preferences and attitudes of a customer, customer learning takes a holistic view of that customer. Avoid the narrow silo questions and ask the broader ones. What are the customer's total needs? What are their personal lifestyle characteristics viewed from within their family context? If you are looking at a business, target your enquiries to understand its complete business. What is the current cash flow picture? Where are the growth opportunities? What financial performance issues are there?

Fourth, in this type of customer research, deep market segmentation defines the group of customers to study. Numerous segmentation variables are used in addition to the common ones mentioned earlier, and the segments can't be labelled using the language frequently used to describe them. They are each so unique the marketer must invent labels to describe them.

For example, the North Shore Credit Union in North Vancouver, B.C., defined two of their high net worth customer segments as 'cruising commuters' and 'urban gentry'. These are certainly not like the common labels referred to earlier; the names themselves imply characteristics unique to the individuals in each segment and also show the creativity of Mike Zywicki, North Shore Credit Union's Senior Manager — Market Segments and Products, who created them.

As another example, at BC Telecom we defined two of our residential market segments as high value and high potential value to differentiate between the revenue sources of each. High value referred to customers that generated high revenue today, whereas high *potential* value captured those customers who had the potential to produce significant revenue for us in the future.

Customer learning studies small groups of customers to reach a deep understanding of each person in the group.

Lastly, by not using traditional market research but evaluating the entire group of customers in terms of many segmentation variables, you end up deriving a multitude of small segments and, as a result, you know a great deal about each person in the segment. The more segmentation variables used, the deeper the insights into the people in the segments. A typical profile is replaced with a more unique one.

QUICK HITS

Customer Learning

■ Learns continuously who your customers are and what they want.

■ Engages all employees in the learning process.

■ Looks at the customer holistically to discover their total needs, wants and expectations.

■ Involves segmentation using many variables to gain a more detailed understanding of what each person in the segment looks like; what their unique characteristics, needs and wants are.

■ Few use it. It is *Different.*

In the example used previously, additional information on each person in the V4A 4A4 postal code in B.C. would be gathered if we simply added segmentation variables such as sex, age, income and profession. The original single segment with a low customer learning quotient suddenly is morphed into ten customer groups, each different from the other but homogeneous within. And the learning quotient has been increased by a factor of at least ten.

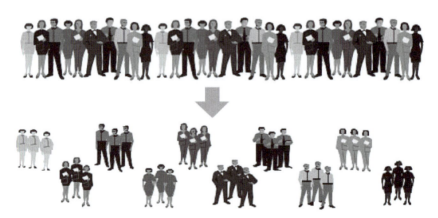

Referring back to the North Shore Credit Union example, here are the definitions they created for two of their high net worth customer segments. Clearly they understood that in order to get a rich understanding of the individuals in each group they needed to use a number of segmentation variables. As you read the description of each segment, try to picture each person.

Cruising Commuters

'A commuting culture has emerged along the expressways linking metropolitan areas with their surrounding suburbs. Combining affordable housing with good jobs, these early to rise and early to bed families may juggle their schedules but at the end of the day they enjoy some suburban peace. Their average household income of $94,000 should easily pay for auto repairs and a new tire or two. Cruising commuters index high on homes built in the 1970s, single detached houses, and recent inter-provincial migration.'

Urban Gentry

'Some well-to-do urban neighbourhoods are modest in lifestyle, though quite economically secure. Urban gentry exemplifies a more conservative lifestyle compared to some of their high-flying neighbours, though their interests may range from foreign travel to the local jazz scene. An average household income of $96,000 will also buy a lot of theatre tickets. Urban gentry indexes high on older homes built in the late 1950s and 1960s, university education, and managerial employment.'

Even though these examples pertain to a smaller financial institution in B.C., there is no reason why similar results can't be achieved for any organization of any size.

How deep should you segment your market? In the example of the V4A 4A4 postal code in B.C. segment, how many more distinct customer groups beyond ten should we try to identify? Some would say that the ultimate conclusion to this process is to get to segments of one (see following figure).

Large Homogeneous Segments

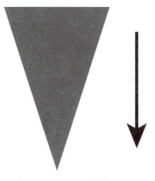

Segments of One

This would mean that you have discovered the uniqueness of each of your customers to the point where you can describe each one in detail. In the earlier example this means we would define thirty unique segments of one to serve as the driver for all marketing Be Different activity. Many would claim that this is impractical, that the investment required to differentiate marketing programs for each of the thirty segments would not warrant doing it. It's a myth. In the foreword to *Permission Marketing* by Seth Godin, marketing guru Don Peppers, president and founder of Marketing 1.1 Inc., says this:

> 'Today, because of interactive technology, it has become cost-efficient once again to conduct individual dialogues, even with millions of consumers — one customer at a time … consumers can, once again, be involved in the marketing process … Marketing in an interactive world is a collaborative activity … with the marketer helping the consumer to buy and the consumer helping the marketer to sell.'

So, if the technology exists to define and market to segments of one, what other considerations should influence the decision to go there? For most organizations, there is the practicality of doing it. It is expressed in a variety of ways: 'It doesn't make any sense to try to define 100,000 segments of one in our business. We could never market to each of them.' Or, 'The complexity of trying to develop a marketing program for 1.5 million customer segments would be a nightmare; it would never work.'

Whatever your organization's mindset and circumstance, it is most important that you use deep segmentation to discover *customer differences*. Keep segmenting your market until you have a sufficient number of segments to understand the different characteristics of each. You may never get to segments of one, but if you increase the number of segments by a factor of ten, as in our previous example, you are miles ahead of where you would have been and miles ahead of your competition.

A market segment of one: perhaps the impossible dream, but embark on the journey and discover Be Different marketing.

Here's another way to look at the segmentation issue. If you can easily label the segments you have defined, you probably don't have enough of them. The easier it is to label them, implying that you are describing broad categories of customers, the less you will know about each person in each of the segments and the less value the customer knowledge will be to create Be Different marketing programs. So, get marketers to keep on segmenting. Discover customer differences.

Finally, few organizations use the customer learning method as opposed to traditional market research. So the approach by definition is Different.

QUICK HITS

■ Remember the key differences between market research and customer learning.

Market Research	Customer Learning
Evaluates the market periodically	Is an ongoing process
Is done by an external firm	Engages all employees
Is viewed as a study	Is considered a core competency of the firm
Takes a snapshot of customer in time	Looks at the customer continually
Takes a narrow view of the customer	Looks at the customer holistically
Describes a typical/average customer	Understands small customer groups
Uses a few segmentation variables	Uses many segmentation variables
Defines few homogeneous segments	Discovers many homogeneous segments
Knows little about individuals	Has in-depth understanding of customers
Creates easy to label segments	Requires creative labeling to capture distinctiveness of segments
Has limited Be Different potential	Has unlimited opportunity to Be Different
Is used by everyone	Is used by few. It's Different

How do you achieve the benefits of customer learning? It needs to be adopted throughout your organization; it needs to be a way of life for everyone. Declare customer learning as a core competency of the business, give it the highest priority, assign the required resources to get it done, and put it into the leadership performance and compensation plans.

In most cases investments will have to be made. This can range from requiring sophisticated CRM technologies all the way down to simple paper-based systems that capture, store and manipulate data, retrieving it when needed.

Adopt customer learning throughout your organization and make it a way of life for everyone.

Learning behaviors and *learning productivity,* the amount of customer information an employee gathers in a specific time period, must form part of all job descriptions. Internal communications should emphasize what the organization has learned this month, who the employee *learning heroes* are and what they achieved.

Learning must matter in the organization for it to truly become a fundamental fabric of the company's Be Different strategy. Be sure to hold marketing, sales and customer service departments accountable for applying the information learned to improve their effectiveness and productivity. New products and services, differentiated levels of customer service and relationship building should all be derived from customer learning information.

Chapter Twenty-Four

Practical Ways to Implement Customer Learning

It is one thing to talk about the principles of customer learning; but since the theme of this book is the practical application of these principles, we need to turn this brave idea into practical suggestions for implementing them. This chapter is divided into two sections: first, learning about the customer by augmenting traditional research with ongoing information that you can capture through the many customer contact points in your organization, and second, studying and understanding customer purchase behavior.

Ask the customer. Be a sponge to absorb every piece of customer information that you can.

Ask the Customer

The essence of the *ask the customer* approach is to open your organization to the customer. Invite the customer to come on in and take part in creating your future. Present your organization as eager to learn how well it is serving its customers, always anxious to do better for them.

On a scale of one to ten, where does your organization rate on this approach? A high score says that you understand the importance of being open to customers and learning from them; a low score suggests that you are closed for business and aren't learning oriented.

Whatever your score, there are tremendous opportunities to develop a stronger customer learning culture by asking your customers direct questions not only through traditional customer research methods but also through the normal daily contact you have with them. Every time your customers, or prospective ones, come in contact with your organization in some way, there is an opportunity to learn something about them — if you have customer learning in mind.

Every customer contact must be engineered not only to meet customers' needs at that particular moment, such as obtaining information about a product or service or determining your store hours, it must also provide information that can be put to effective marketing use. So, the takeaway for you is to not think about a customer contact as only a transaction or a service interaction, but as a strategic opportunity in which you have the potential to learn something that will truly separate your organization from the pack, if you choose to take advantage of it.

A customer contact is a moment of strategic opportunity to learn something that will separate your organization from the pack.

In addition, learning through observation is an effective way to glean valuable customer information from daily customer encounters. You don't always have to ask questions; watch, learn and record what you hear and see.

There are a variety of sources in your organization that will provide you with the rich and robust customer information you require. Utilize every one. Get your employees talking to one another to share what they are learning. Here are some specific examples.

- Engage all of your customer contact employees. They have the potential to collect amazing information about your customers every time they speak to one. They have quality time with your customers. As stated earlier, the key is to design each customer contact to extract the critical information you need. So, for example, when a customer calls a billing representative, what information would typically be available through that interaction? What are the normal questions the representative could ask? Your questions must be designed with the customer in mind. You don't want to force questions on the customer; you want them to be a natural extension of the dialogue taking place. If it is an unnatural query on your part it will likely be uncomfortable for the customer and will not illicit the response you want or the information you need.

Try this approach: First, define each customer service interaction in your organization; then define the learning outcome you want from each; and finally, design the list of questions that will elicit the information you require. More importantly, you also need to constantly reinforce the importance of gathering the learning information all the time.

For each customer service interaction, define the learning outcomes and design the list of questions that will get the information you require.

To do this, make customer learning an integral part of the employee's performance plan for which they are held accountable. Review the information they collect from customers on a regular basis; coach them to do better and reward them when they excel.

To make this process successful, however, it must be easy and simple for the customer service employee to participate. If the system is not clear and straightforward, employees will simply not engage.

- Use your website to gather information about customers. What kind of information are they seeking? Are customers researching product information? Do they want to buy something? Are they looking for a contact? Are they willing to share their personal information with you? The answers to these questions should inform your web learning strategy.

- Direct mail campaigns are an excellent source for learning about your customers. Design them with this in mind. Even though your primary purpose is to inform your customers of new products or to sell them something, always be thinking of how to extract as much information from this contact as you can. If you are asking the customer to respond to the mailing, see if you can get them to give you other information about themselves as well that might be useful. Each contact is an opportunity to learn. Maximize it.

- Customer communication via e-mail has great learning potential. Every message coming to you through your website Contact Us button can yield substantial benefits if you have customer learning in mind when you design the communication. If customers e-mail you to get help regarding some aspect of your business they are currently engaged in, what is your communications strategy? The reply needs to get back as soon as possible. Time is of the essence, and if you don't reply to an e-mail in two days the message you are giving the customer is clearly 'We don't care about you and your message to us was a pain.' A quick reply will earn you the right to ask for more information from the customer since he will be leaning your way. Establish the information you can reasonably obtain from this type of contact and give it a try every time.

- Invoices sent to customers. Customers review this personal document carefully. They are giving an organization their undivided attention for the time they are assessing the bill and determining if it is correct. Learning strategy demands that every communication with the customer be looked upon as an opportunity, so design the invoice with this in mind. It should include the bill format, the content, and a section for the customer to communicate back to you, perhaps by e-mail, if they choose to do so. Also, did you ever consider asking specific questions on your invoice such as whether your prices are reasonable, is the customer aware of new products available and then perhaps is there some personal information, such as likes and dislikes, that would help the company serve them better?

- What about customer complaints as a source of customer learning? Does your organization ever get any of these? This could be a letter or a phone call — in which case, the person handling the complaint call has a list of questions to ask — or an e-mail; the source really doesn't matter. What matters is that a customer is complaining about something they don't like about you. What a great learning opportunity. Unfortunately, many employees simply don't like responding to customer complaints. It often can be a painful and frustrating process for an employee who can see little or no obvious benefit or satisfaction in dealing with dissatisfied customers.

Most employees don't like handling customer complaints — but what an incredible learning source!

From the customer's viewpoint, a typical response to a complaint that simply quotes policy is not helpful at all since it probably was the policy that upset the customer in the first place. Have the learning attitude in mind as you design your customer complaint process. Here are some ideas that will help you transform this painful event into an investment in customer learning that will yield handsome returns.

- Get back to the customer immediately. A sense of urgency on your part demonstrates caring to the customer. If you don't have the answer for the customer right away and it will take a week to get it, tell them. You need to at least acknowledge that you have heard the complaint. Perhaps you can even extract more information on the nature of the problem, showing that you are doing something about it.

- As I said earlier, don't quote internal policy as your response. If your policy is the theme of your response, you will upset the customer even more and you will preempt your ability to get useful learning information from them now and in the future. Your reply has to smell like problem solving, which is what you are trying to do in this situation. If you can solve the customer's problem and not quote company policy you have gained the customer's respect and confidence. Maybe you can even add to your repository of customer learning.

– Furthermore, the nature of your response to a complaint goes a long way in defining the openness of your organization. To be able to acknowledge that the customer has a valid point of view and admit that your organization might actually be trying to enforce a policy that makes little sense to them shows that you are aware of their plight and willing to change to address it with them.

– Ensure that your reply is customer friendly in terms of dealing with the emotional triggers that are at play here. An upset customer doesn't want to be buried in your logic; they want to feel that you care about their problem and that you are honestly trying to help.

– Record what you have learned about this customer from this interaction, and look closer at the complaint reply message. If this is one of your valued clients, why not make a good old fashioned phone call to them? Consider having a senior manager make the call. This personal attention will be well received and is well worth the effort.

Don't quote internal policy to complaining customers unless you want them more angry.

A respected colleague, Lorne Armstrong (www.armstrongresults. com) tells me of a Total Customer Commitment seminar he attended sponsored by NORPAC Controls (www.norpaccontrols. com), a B.C. company. NORPAC has been in the instrumentation and process control business since 1972. The company has a *Be the Customer* vision, a total customer commitment culture; it certainly has its act together in understanding the importance of customer complaints and what can be learned from them. The organization believes that it takes a very special person to take customer complaints, and it wants this type of an employee as part of its service team.

Its way of making handling complaints matter and monitoring its progress in developing incredible team *complaint getters* is to measure right down to the individual how many complaints are received and successfully handled. What an arsenal of customer information they have through this process. How many companies do you know that have this kind of Be Different insight? NORPAC is truly unique.

Great employees attract complaining customers!

I raised the IT systems implications of collecting customer information earlier and a question you might be asking here is 'How do I organize all of the information collected from the myriad of sources available to me in a way that is practical?' Good question. If you have a small business, for example, you might not be willing to invest in a more sophisticated Customer Relationship Management (CRM) system to do the job.

Later in this chapter we will explore the specific marketing support we need from information technology, but in the meantime don't let the systems challenges decide whether or not you collect valuable customer information. The Be Different approach is to declare that getting to know your customers will be a core competency of your organization, and then figure out how to do it in your way.

QUICK HITS

■ There are two practical ways to implement customer learning: ask the customer and understand customer behavior.

■ The ask-the-customer approach is to literally open up your organization and invite the customer in. Be an active listener, eager to get whatever information you can from a customer by whatever means possible.

■ Look to every customer contact point to gather customer information. Design the contact to give you as much information as possible.

■ Treat a customer contact as a moment of strategic opportunity.

■ Use customer complaints as learning vehicles and honor those employees who attract complaining customers.

Twitter is the most practical way I've seen to get started up the customer learning curve. It's free, easy to set up and gives you the ability to start immediately building relationships with people who are important to your organization. Companies such as Ford, Southwest Airlines, the Red Cross and the Marriott International Hotels and Resorts are active tweeters with their customers, learning useful information from them on their operations. Suggestions for improvement, service complaints and product feedback are areas that provide a fertile customer-learning environment.

Understanding Customer Behavior

In addition to the ask-the-customer method of customer learning, you can also obtain rich information about them by tracking their purchasing behavior: how they use the products and services that you provide. Behavioral tracking on a particular customer is a method of gathering information such as what products are purchased, how frequently they are purchased, when they are purchased, what other products are purchased at the same time, what products are being substituted and what products are being dropped.

Rich information on customers can be obtained by tracking the way in which they consume your products and services.

This information can then be used to develop a profile of a customer with specific product usage patterns which could then be used to target a similar package of products to other customers. For example, if tracking data showed that when a customer bought high speed Internet service they also bought a wireless modem, you could use this knowledge to offer the two services together as a package to other customers with similar profiles.

On a more sophisticated level, behavior tracking information can be used to develop models that can predict how a group of customers with predetermined product or service usage characteristics will react to being presented with another specific type of offer. For example, in the Internet + wireless modem example above, it is possible to construct a model that predicts with a certain level of certainty the likelihood that a customer buying Internet service will also take a wireless modem.

In the BC Telecom world, we discovered that for certain residential customer segments there was a strong predictive correlation between the customer's use of long distance services and the likelihood of their purchasing other more discretionary services like Specialty phones and such custom network services as call number identification, call waiting and call alert. We designed our marketing campaigns around this knowledge by targeting direct mail programs for these additional phone and network products and services to customers with higher long distance bills. Our outbound tele-marketing calls were targeted as well.

Turbocharge your behavioral data with predictive models.

To give you an idea of some of generic sources for understanding customer behavior, here is a potential list:

- Customer product and service usage

- Customer current revenues

- Customer loyalty (how long someone has been a customer)

- Customer past revenue history

- Customer contracts

- Customer channel buying preferences

- Customer credit history

- Competition in the customer's business

- Repair history

- Sales campaigns response history

QUICK HITS

■ The second approach to implementing customer learning is to gain an in-depth understanding of how customers use your products and services.

■ Behavioral tracking combined with predictive modeling can provide great insights into relationship building and selling opportunities.

■ In addition, customer usage data can be used to segment your customer base. One of the simplest approaches is to segment your customers on the basis of how much revenue they give you.

■ Separate your high spenders from your low spenders as one means of determining where to focus your attention.

Which organizations are proficient in customer learning? Who does it well? Unfortunately, few organizations use the ask-the-customer approach and formally capture customer information from a variety of customer contact points; this is, on the one hand, disappointing, but, on the other, a tremendous opportunity for you to Be Different.

The North Shore Credit Union (NSCU) in North Vancouver, B.C., however, has taken a bold step in this direction. They have created a *membership relationship management* system that, although in its infancy, is driven by a vision to leverage customer learning as a key competitive element in its overall strategic game plan. The technology platform the credit union selected allows it to capture customer information in real time and in a free record format, making it easy for frontline employees to record customer feedback in conversation with them. This is intended to make information available to their marketers for new services development and to their branch staff to monitor the member interaction experience. NSCU is a relatively small financial institution with a big idea when it comes to being successful in this highly competitive market.

Few organizations use the ask-the-customer approach; disappointing, but an opportunity to Be Different.

Reg Marrinier, VP Retail Banking, puts it this way: 'The financial services marketplace is highly saturated and extremely competitive. The key for businesses facing these same circumstances is turning data into wisdom. When you can translate that wisdom into the client experience, you have won. You will have created significant barriers to entry and a differentiated client experience that others will not be able to replicate.' Every bold idea needs Be Different leadership. Good for them.

The learning tool most organizations use, however, seems to be the *understanding customer behavior* method. I am sure that you have received direct mail advertising from a company with whom you are currently doing business inviting you to join its loyalty program, book a hotel in New York, upgrade to a new and improved credit card and so on. Behind all of these programs is a system that has at least tracked your product usage and may have predicted that you would be interested in purchasing additional products and services. I regularly receive offers from my bank to extend the credit limit on my Visa card, to switch to an elite Visa card with more privileges and lower interest rates or to invest in a low risk investment management product. This ability to offer such additional services is possible only because I have been doing business with this bank for many years and they have obviously tracked my behavior and likelihood to respond to these additional offers.

Tracking how customers use products and services defines customer learning for most organizations.

As vice president of marketing and sales for BC Telecom, I developed sophisticated tools to deepen our understanding of our residential mass market customers and to leverage customer usage information and provide targeted telecom packages for them. The learning process started with defining the specific business objectives we wanted to achieve and then using a market segmentation approach with as many segmentation variables around how customers used our services as we could practically consider.

My thanks to Terry Taciuk, the former director of customer marketing, for his leadership in developing this initiative, and for his significant contribution to changing the marketing culture of the organization.

The variables that we chose to segment our markets included:

- Current customer behavior – This included information about each customer such as current revenue, product usage, community of interest (where did they call long distance?), customer loyalty (how long have they been with us?), geography (where did they reside?), and credit history (did they pay their bills regularly?).

- Potential future value and risk – In Section Two we discussed the concept of the lifetime value of a customer and said that it was a combination of both the current value you receive from a customer and the strategic or potential value you expect to generate from the customer in the future. This future value aspect of a customer was an important segmentation variable in our work at BC Telecom; we derived it from predictive modeling algorithms and we modified it by assessing the risk that a customer presented by virtue of their credit history.

For example, a customer with a high future value potential combined with a negative credit history produced a lower final value result to the organization. To understand the investment risk to the company, we needed to understand both sides of the equation: were they likely to be interested in a particular offer, and would they pay for it?

- Demographic and psychographic overlays – In our case, we chose to overlay these attributes on the current behavior and potential value information of each customer.

- Ask-the-customer research/surveys/feedback – To enhance the richness of our customer understanding, needs, expectations, attitudes and preferences were collected on each customer and added to the mix of product and service data.

Keep searching for sub-groups in your customer segments to enhance the learning process.

Using these segmentation variables against our total number of residential customers in B.C., we were able to assign individuals to the following groups that were different from each other but homogeneous within:

- High Current Value Group – representing 25% of the customers and 44% of the monthly revenue

- High Potential Value Group – 66% of the customers; 46% of the revenue

- New Customer Group – new residents of the province who clearly had unique characteristics and needs differing from other consumers. This group constituted 7% of the consumer base and 8% of the monthly revenues

- Home Business Group – consumers with home-based businesses and different telecommunications requirements. They were only 2% of the consumers, substantially higher today with the increasing trend for people to work from home, and generated 2% of the revenue

We went further and defined multiple sub-groups for each of these segments in order to enhance the learning process. This segmentation approach was not only extremely helpful in enriching our customer learning, it also was instrumental in changing the culture of our marketing organization.

The product-driven approach gradually gave way to the customerized approach which was accepted as the way of doing business in the marketing division. BC Telecom was recognized by the BC Chapter of the American Marketing Association as the Marketer of the Year in 1998, due in large measure to the work we had done in customer learning.

To summarize our approach, the customer segmentation toolbox we used consisted of the following:

- Predictive models – looking for the selling opportunities with the highest probability of success

- Current and future potential – calculating the lifetime value of the customer

- Behavioral segmentation – segmenting the customer base using behavioral data from a wide range of company sources alluded to above

- Ask-the-customer data – enriching the behavioral data with customer learning information from market research studies and other internal information sources

- Segmentation map – creating segmentation categories for each segment

■ Think about customer learning as having three dimensions:

- Segmentation process – deep segmentation to define a large number of unique clusters of customers providing detailed insight into the characteristics of the individuals in the cluster

- Ask the customer – understanding the customer by capturing information from the numerous customer contact points in an organization as well as through traditional customer research

- Understanding customer behavior – gaining insights into the customer from tracking information that describes the way in which they engage with your organization on an ongoing basis

Chapter Twenty-Five

Customer Secrets: The New Marketing Power

Instituting customer learning processes in an organization is a solid first step to creating Be Different marketing but there is much more to do to leverage this capability. The next challenge is to determine what type of information you want to gather on each of your customers. Words such as needs, wants, expectations, characteristics and requirements describe the nature of the information we want to gather on customers. To that list, I offer a crucial addition.

Everyone determines customer needs; enlightened Be Different marketing is to discover the innermost secrets of a customer.

Whereas traditional marketing says that you should focus on determining the needs of your customer, the Be Different approach is to discover the secrets of each and every customer. This approach is powerful in terms of the potential impact on your organization because most organizations simply do not understand it. Most marketing teams still practice traditional marketing; there is nothing wrong with this but it simply doesn't go far enough. There is nothing unique about the marketing practice of focusing on customer needs; marketing enlightenment and organizational opportunity come from discovering customers' deepest innermost desires.

Let's differentiate between the two concepts.

A Customer Need

First, a customer need is determined from a high level of understanding of a particular group of customers. As discussed in the Customer Learning chapter, traditional segmentation methodology produces a small number of relatively large segments of customers, due to the few segmentation variables used. As a result, it is limited in the depth of information gathered on each customer in the segment. It provides a profile of what the typical customers look like in the segment and what their needs may be.

A customer need is product-centric; a customer secret is personal-centric.

Second, a customer need is typically product-centric. Needs are derived from the buckets of products and services that are commonplace in the market today. For example, we need financing for our home, work and family transportation, recreational choices, home entertainment, and a means of communicating with business associates, family and friends. In this sense, a need is tangible and relates to the features of a product or service designed to satisfy it.

A Customer Secret

A customer secret, on the other hand, is a detailed personal level of understanding of a single customer arrived at through successive segmentation to define smaller and smaller groups of customers. Additional segmentation variables are added to gain richer and richer insights into the attitudes, preferences and characteristics of customers and their specific consumption habits.

The secret discovery process builds on this idea by requiring that, as you learn more about a particular group of customers, you need to leverage what you have learned to determine additional segmentation variables to the point where the segment derived becomes so small that it approaches a segment of one. Remember, the point is not whether or not you actually get to segments of one, rather that its driving concept be lived in the marketing organization: deep segmentation is good; deeper is Different.

Secrets-driven discovery unlocks the power of your marketing efforts.

As personal-centric, a customer secret is a fundamental part of a customer's persona. Secrets could include such information as:

- I am in a high-pressured job.

- I earn a $60,000 salary and have a limited amount of vacation time.

- I like to plan things well in advance.

- I demand a lifestyle free from hassle.

- I have a family of four.

- I love Italian food and wine.

- I love to ski.

- I drive an SUV.

In these examples, note the use of the first person, 'I.' Ultimately this is where you want to end up, but you may reach an interim point where you are able to identify a small group of customers who share similar secrets. If you do, you are miles ahead of your competitors who have stopped at the needs definition stage and as a result have achieved no differentiated position in the market.

You can see the power of the secrets dimension of customer knowledge when you first segment your market into many small clusters of customers and then go beyond product-based needs to personal-based secrets. You literally unlock the potential of your marketing efforts. You now have rich and robust customer intelligence that can be used in so many ways in your organization to improve the way you serve customers, how you sell to them or what marketing programs you offer them. Not only that, you are now in possession of information that few, if any, of your competitors have. How cool is that? Does it give an organization the power to Be Different? You bet.

Leverage the intimate understanding of customers; be competitively unmatched.

I referred earlier to a rather creative financial services business in western Canada that, as part of its HOW to WIN strategic game plan, would develop the capability to leverage its intimate understanding of customers. Management's assessment was that no other supplier of financial services to wealthy individuals in their marketplace was researching with enough depth to understand the non-financial secrets of these individuals. They furthermore reasoned that gathering and applying this information in a marketing-smart way would mean they would be competitively unmatched.

They liked the word *insights* rather than secrets and they implemented a series of customer learning tools, including Internet surveys and traditional focus groups, to gather the information they needed. They decided to focus on learning where these more wealthy customers chose to do business in their daily lives. Specifically, they looked at the following categories: grocery stores, restaurants, service stations, retail stores and leisure activities.

These are examples of the insights they discovered:

- In the grocery category, the most popular place the target customers shopped was the Snug Cove store, followed by the Ruddy Potato Market. It was interesting that the major chain stores such as Canada Safeway and Save-On-Foods were down the list in terms of popularity.

- In the restaurant category, these customers frequented the local Starbucks; the second most popular place was Subway.

- In terms of their leisure time, these people liked to spend their hard-earned cash at the local wellness center and the recreational ski area, followed by Rogers Video and the B.C. Ferry Service.

This perspective into customer habits was extremely valuable. The organization was able to paint a picture of what the high net worth individual in a geographic region of Greater Vancouver looked like in terms of these specific lifestyle dimensions and then develop customerized marketing programs targeted at customers reflecting this valuable information. Admittedly, this profile is not complete; additional lifestyle categories and segmentation variables would have to be added as the organization learns more and more about this particular segment.

QUICK HITS

■ Remember the key differences between a customer need and a customer secret:

Customer Need	Customer Secret
High level of understanding	Detailed level of understanding
Focus is on groups of people	Focus is on the individual
Product-centric: it, the product	Personal-centric: I, the person

Chapter Twenty-Six

Holistic Offers: The Total Customer Counts

So how do you transform secret information into marketing power?

Rather than selling individual products to a mass market, the customerized approach develops packaged offers for small groups of customers. I want to advance the packaged notion further, given the opportunities made available to marketers by discovering customer secrets.

Use customer needs-plus-secrets to create holistic offers for your chosen customers.

Given the personal centricity of secrets, whether of an individual or a business organization, and the scope of customer value they promise, we should consider a term that is more appropriate to the whole person or organization as opposed to a narrow set of their needs that can be satisfied by packaging products and services together.

My term for this is *holistic offer*. And in order to get a clear understanding of the idea, we have to differentiate it from traditional product packaging.

Product Package

A product, as discussed in Chapter Twenty-One, is based on a narrowly defined feature set which in most cases is determined by technological attributes. For example, Internet access has speed characteristics, a DVD player either has or does not have HD capability and a mobile phone has a personal locator capability or not.

When you package a number of products together, it is a challenge to create a synergistic value proposition that reflects the total value derived from the collective products in the package. That challenge is to take a number of technologically driven product features and somehow derive a common value theme that can be expressed by the sum of them.

If you package products together, develop a unique value proposition that creates synergy for the product components and don't resort to using price to market it.

For example, what is the value proposition to the customer when you package together home phone service and high speed Internet? Bundling voice service with Internet data service produces what combined value? In most cases it is easier — and almost always done — to resort to price, and say 'take a bundle of both services and get a 10% discount.' This approach is limited in creating additional value and can be easily copied by competitors.

It is possible to create a common value theme by packaging products and services together. In fact, if you determined that customers typically purchase a number of products together, it certainly would suggest that these products deliver some aggregate value and should therefore be considered a potential holistic offer. In the next chapter, I will discuss this approach, but I want to caution you at this point that if you choose to package products and services together, it is only successful if you develop a *unique value proposition* that creates a synergistic theme for the product components. More importantly, do not resort to using price as a way to market them.

Let's test you on the holistic product concept. Here is a multiple choice question:

| A | B | (A) + (B) | (A+B) |

The first choice, (A) + (B), implies that you are adding the value from product A to the value from product B; the second choice, (A+B), implies that you create new value by combining the value attributes of each product. In this case (A+B) is the correct answer.

Holistic Offer

On the other hand, a holistic offer is inherently broad in nature. It provides a wide range of customer value created by considering all of the needs plus secrets that you discover about a customer. It is an extremely liberating and flexible marketing concept that can go wherever you want it to go given the secrets uncovered. If you have discovered ten meaningful and relevant secrets for a particular group of customers, the holistic offer can respond to all ten; if the secret count is five, the holistic offer can be smaller. In other words, the dimensions of a holistic offer are a function of the number of secrets discovered. Think of it as a broad collection of values and not just a few specific ones that are important to a customer.

As opposed to a number of features that packaged products provide, an offer consists of many *capabilities.* A capability can be a product or service and it can also include services like billing, sales support and customer service. In addition, a capability can also be a product or service offered by another organization. Consideration of an external capability in your holistic offer would be appropriate if the needs-plus-secrets information required you to obtain value that you currently don't provide. For example, if you were in the airline business and needed a hotel value component for a holistic offer, you would most likely approach an accommodation business to see if they would be willing to provide the hotel component.

A holistic offer provides a wide range of customer value created by the needs-plus-secrets you have discovered. It is a collection of value not a thin slice.

In terms of the customer value proposition, packaging products or services is a bottom-up process that takes the value provided by the various individual products in the package and develops a common value thread that brings them all together. Creating a value proposition for a holistic offer, on the other hand, is more of a top-down approach. It is created from the set of customer needs plus secrets discovered and expresses the value that you are providing.

Here's an example that illustrates the way in which needs plus secrets can be integrated into a holistic offer. Let's say that your organization is in the business of providing ski vacations, and you have defined the following characteristics of your target market segment:

- Males dominate the segment and are the decision makers in taking ski vacations.

- Average age group is 40 to 50.

- The Greater Vancouver area of B.C. has a significant concentration of males aged between 40 and 50.

In addition to the above, let's say that you discovered the following secrets about your target male customers:

- I earn $60,000 and have a limited amount of vacation time.

- I like to plan things well in advance.

- I demand a hassle-free lifestyle.

- I have a family of four.

- I love Italian food and wine.

- I love to ski.

- I drive an SUV.

- I am an executive under extreme job pressure.

You now have the ability to define several capabilities of a ski package offer and to challenge other organizations to match you. You could design your holistic offer to include:

- Three days of skiing at Blackcomb Mountain in Whistler, B.C.

- Two nights' accommodation at the Fairmont Chateau Whistler

- Dinner for four at Umberto's, probably the finest Italian restaurant in Whistler

- Ski camp experiences for the children

- Valet vehicle detailing upon arrival

Wrap all these dimensions up in an offer branded 'The Ultimate Weekend Ski Experience', target it specifically to those people you have discovered to have the same needs-plus-secrets set, and you just might have a winner.

What competition would you expect? Significant competition would be minimal due to the high degree of customization as well as the nucleus of secrets used to build the package. Without the secret set would this be as potent an offering? Not likely, as it would be more narrowly defined and would provide less customer value.

One last point: To create the above offer, would you necessarily have to be in the ski vacation business? No. The truth is that you could develop and market this offer if you were in any business. All you need is to piggyback secrets on needs and create a compelling value proposition. You could do this, for example, if you were in the restaurant or hotel business as well.

Creating holistic offers places you in the value integration business; piggyback secrets on needs and create a compelling value proposition.

What is involved is integrating a number of components needed to produce the final offer. In this respect the marketing role is one of systems integration: pulling a number of disparate parts into one cohesive package to deliver a relevant and compelling value proposition for the targeted customer.

Consider the following real life examples of holistic offers:

A former boss and mentor, Bill McCourt, developed an intriguing offer during his tenure as the senior marketing executive for a large retail department store in Vancouver. The value proposition was to create a special customer experience on every floor of the store. For example, on the second floor, which was women's fashions, $2,000 worth of core store merchandise was offered and was enveloped by a very unique experience:

- You and your favorite person were picked up from your home in a limousine and were taken to the store after normal business hours.

- You were taken to the second floor, where the best salesperson in each department along with a fashion coordinator and tailor were standing by.

- You had two hours to buy $2,000 worth of merchandise.

- Afterwards you were taken by limo to your favorite restaurant.

In this case, the store was prepared to invest some of the profit margin from the merchandise sold to finance the attendant costs of the offer, the limo rental and restaurant meal costs. Bill tells me that even though the offer did not blow away the banker, it went a long way to create intense employee excitement and great publicity for the store.

I discovered another holistic offer while shopping for Christmas gifts for my grandchildren at Toys 'R' Us in Vancouver. Diamond Parking Service (www.diamondparking.ca), which operates the store parking facility, created an interesting proposition for those people parking in its lot.

The offer is called 'Discover the Difference. Diamond Parking's We Care Program'. Here is the verbatim quote from the sign that overlooks their facility:

> 'We provide these services FREE when you park with us:
>
> 1. Retrieve keys locked in car
>
> 2. Inflate a flat or install a spare
>
> 3. Jump start a dead battery
>
> 4. Supply enough gas to reach the nearest 24-hour gas station'

Interesting value proposition: Park in our lot for a reasonable price and if you return to your car and are greeted with an unexpected surprise — you locked your keys in your car, you have a flat tire, your car won't start due to a dead battery or no gas left in the tank — we will take care of you. This company made the decision to underwrite the costs of the emergency services it may infrequently have to provide as part of their standard parking rates. Even considering the potential pitfalls of offering value for free, it's an impressive offer.

The Athens Marriott Ledra gave me an offer that blew me away on a recent memorable stay. Their experience package included things like an unmatched 8th floor view fo the Acropolis, personalized room service — you get to pick the time you want your room made up, a *say yes* attitude — we showed up at 9am after getting off a cruise ship and they checked us in; we asked for flowers for some friends and they found them and had them dellivered to our room precisely when they promised, THE best beds in the world — a distinguishable difference in comfort between the Marriott and any other hotel, multiple power outlets in each room with 110 and 220 service to accommodate their international guests, a *Ledra Business Package* — for 49 Euros you get breakfast for two, unlimited high speed internet access and mini-bar contents — water, soft drinks, wine and beer, and personalized guest communications — messages on the TV asking if we were interested in having them arrange for airport taxi service on the specific day we were leaving; a competitive fixed rate to avoid any surprises and to make it easy for us to pay for the service on our hotel bill.

QUICK HITS

■ Remember the key differences between a product package and a holistic offer.

Product Package	Holistic Offer
Needs driven	Piggybacks secrets on top of needs
Features drive benefits	Unique value proposition creates benefits
Bottom-up value based on features and benefits	Top-down value proposition
Made up of features	Composed of capabilities
Narrow benefits provided	Broad range of value created
Technology driven	Integration of an array of capabilities

Chapter Twenty-Seven

Practical Ways to Implement a Holistic Offer

What about practical and proven ways to actually develop an offer? In this chapter I will describe two approaches that leverage how we implement customer learning covered in Chapters Twenty-Three and Twenty-Four: *asking the customer* and *understanding customer behavior.*

Offer Creation Method #1 — Ask the Customer

This approach builds an offer utilizing the information you have gathered about your customers from an array of sources including traditional market research and the many customer contact points in your organization. Of course, this assumes you have done your segmentation work to define the group of customers that represents the best strategic opportunity for your business. Here's the process:

1. **Create a customer attributes map**

    Use the needs plus secrets information that you have gathered on your targeted customers. This involves constructing a scatter diagram displaying each individual need and secret and then grouping these in a logical way to define the value components to be provided. This process doesn't have to be complicated. Take a blank padboard sheet of paper and paste a Post-it Note to it for each need and secret that you have identified. Once you have a number of individual notes up on the sheet, look for logical synergistic clusters of this information that relate to the customer value that can be provided. This grouping is a very important step because it shapes the nature of the value proposition being created.

A customer attributes map displays needs-plus-secrets and groups them in value clusters.

Let's do this for an example to give you an idea how it could work. Let's assume that you have uncovered the following needs-plus-secrets profile of the customer group you are assessing:

- male executive

- salary $100K per year

- two weeks per year for vacation

- needs to be in touch with the office while on vacation

- owns an SUV

- married with 1.5 children

- home is over 3,000 square feet in the $1 million range

- no time to maintain home yet wants it well kept at all times

- considers planning a vacation a hassle

- dines out at least three times a week

- loves Italian food and wine

- enjoys water sports for recreation

- favorite vacation destination is Hawaii

- has no time to buy gifts for friends and loved ones

- has $200K invested in wealth management services

- banks at CIBC or the Royal Bank

- uses a personal trainer for fitness

Consider this listing of information as your scatter diagram of customer facts.

The next step is to group these facts into some logical fashion in order to easily define the value to be delivered to the customer. This is a strategic exercise based on the value you want to provide and is based on your particular business and your overall strategy. In this example let's assume that you are in the financial services business.

You could consider the following grouping:

- Financial Services, the anchor of your offer – personal advisor, special interest mortgage and lines of credit

- Household Management Services – home insurance, lawn and garden services, maid service, vehicle insurance

- Telecommunications Services – wireless e-mail service, long distance service

- Personal Services – fitness training, gift buying and vacation planning, including a special Hawaiian vacation packaged with water sports such as parasailing. Moreover, this component could look slightly different for each customer based on additional information that you uncover about that person

- Dining Out Services – restaurant packages, Italian of course, wine tasting invitations

2. Create the unique value proposition

A unique value proposition captures the overall customer benefits being provided; the objective is to make it different from what your competition provides.

In our example we have five value components to succinctly communicate to the customer that must be unique, otherwise we won't Be Different. This is a vital step in the process as it will determine the relationships we need to build in order to deliver some of the capabilities required. Many of the capabilities are not financial services, and can only be provided if relationships with other companies are forged.

Holistic offers are described by a unique value proposition, not by features and benefits.

Consider the following value proposition in our example:

> 'We are the only ones offering a package of personal services enabling you to effectively manage your world. We make it easy for you to work hard and play hard.'

What are we saying about the value that we are offering? The personal is clear. We want to do whatever we can to take care of the busy lifestyle these customers have so that they can reap the benefits of the hard work they endure day after day. There also is the notion of taking control of one's life to eliminate the stress and hassles that come with the busy executive life.

3. Define the capabilities that you need

Define the capabilities necessary to deliver the value proposition.

This step answers the question: 'What do we need to do to make the value proposition come alive?' Since this is a financial services example, we will assume that we already have the mortgage and lines of credit capabilities the offer requires.

There are four other value components, however, that have little to do with financial services. Household management, telecommunications, personal services and dining capabilities must be included in our offer as well.

This is where your relationships with other suppliers in the business community come into play. The process is straightforward.

Decide which suppliers provide the highest quality products and services you need as capabilities. You want to provide the best personal trainer, for example, and the leading telecom service provider. Ideally, it would be desirable if you already had a relationship with your chosen capability suppliers, but this is not always the case. Assign a senior manager to build these needed relationships in order to show the organization that this is indeed a critical marketing activity.

Find partners that offer high value services and insist on superlative performance from them.

QUICK HITS

■ Managing Your Partners

- Delegate the task of developing/managing external relationships to a senior manager. Make the partnership results part of their compensation plan. If the partnerships fail so does the senior manager.

- Choose best-in-class companies to supply your offer components.

- Clearly define what you expect from each partner.

- Develop a performance plan for each partner with regular, formal performance reviews. Dump those that don't perform. Remember you hold the customer relationship; if your partner fails it reflects on you.

- Get customer feedback on the performance of each of your partners using a *customer report card*. Get feedback monthly.

- Define the consequences of non-performance.

- Develop operations processes and procedures and make sure they are customer inspired.

4. Integrate these capabilities into a cohesive go-to-market plan

- Customer communications – how will you advertise and promote the offer?

- Sales – what channels will you use?

- Operations – how will you fill a customer order given the array of operations processes of your partners? This needs to appear seamless to the customer

- Billing – how will you bill the offer? How will you integrate billing information from your partners into your billing platform, and how will you share offer revenue with them?

- Support – how will you provide customer support after the sale is made?

5. Price the offer

Most organizations today provide product and service bundles driven by customer savings. The bundle generally consists of a number of individual products and services purchased together; the more products purchased the bigger the savings.

A leading wireless company in North America, for example, features a bundle that gives the customer the option of taking all or some of four services offered in a specific geographic area: wireless + home phone + portable Internet + Internet phone service. The pricing scheme was:

- Combine two services and save 5%

- Combine three services and save 10%

- Combine four services and save 15%

Although a creative approach to bundling a number of products and services together, it is not consistent with the principles of holistic offer creation. A bundle is driven by offering incentives to the customer to buy more services in return for greater price discounts. A holistic offer, on the other hand, carries a broad value proposition with substantial value to command a premium price.

Since price is a direct reflection of value, it follows that the more value created for the customer the higher the price. In our financial services example there is an incredible amount of value being provided, not only by the individual capabilities provided in the offer but also through the integration provided to bring all of the capabilities together in a convenient and seamless way. In return for making it easy for the customer to obtain relevant and compelling value you want to be able to charge premium prices.

Holistic value based offers are premium priced, they are not discounted. If you offer compelling value, customers should expect premium prices.

If you discover that your target customers are unwilling to pay a premium price you have only two choices:

- Add more value to support the planned price levels or a higher price. You may have overestimated the price vs. value relationship and you may have to re-examine it.

- Remove value components from the offer and reduce prices accordingly. Don't resort to lowering prices unless you are willing to reduce the value provided by removing individual capabilities from the offer. For example, a lower price point might make sense if the offer did not contain a personal services component. Beware, however, as a reduction in the number of value components could have a material impact on the value proposition you have developed for the offer. You may have to reassess it and modify it appropriately to the reduced set of capabilities and then test it. Is it still meaningful to the customer? If not, you have reached the untenable position of having a lower price point for value that is irrelevant to your chosen customer group.

Premium pricing in the bundling world is rarely seen. Most bundles are positioned to provide more value to the customer at discounted prices. This can be confusing to the customer who has been taught to pay more for products and services of higher value. How does that square with bundling in more value but lowering the price? It simply does not.

In today's bundling world, premium pricing is rarely found. Most bundles provide added value at discounted prices.

Some would argue that providing discounted bundles does make sense because it is a way to create *stickiness* with your customers and keep them loyal to you. The problem is that even though your intent is to keep customers by reducing your margins, it seldom happens. Your competitors can copy bundles relatively easily, and matching price is also easy. How many communications companies are capable of offering a bundle with home phone plus Internet service or mobility service or custom network features? How many financial institutions bundle day-to-day banking with a mortgage? How many telecommunications companies bundle voice, data and mobility services? I rest my case. This approach does not provide effective customer stickiness independently because similar products are available everywhere and price discounting can be matched by all.

Here are a few more examples of bundles with good intentions, but missing the pricing point.

I recently visited a restaurant in the Vancouver area and noticed that it was advertising an offer branded as a 'Family Night' involving the Vancouver Giants hockey team. The target customer was a family of four; the value proposed consisted of food, parking and gasoline all wrapped around the hockey game core element. The five component values included:

- Four tickets to any weekend hockey game

- One game-night parking pass

- Two adult burger meals

- Two children's meals

- One $5.00 gas coupon

This was a very well positioned bundle, integrating the most obvious services a family would use in attending a game. The offer was advertised at $85, an amazing price point considering what people spend on a night out for hockey with the Vancouver Canucks; not exactly the same product, but for comparative purposes a family of four would spend well over $250 for the night's game, including food, gas and parking.

What caught my attention initially was the advertising stating that the value of the offer was $125. So even though the restaurant invested time and money to develop this offer, a substantial value to their targeted customer group, it not only discount-priced it but openly acknowledged that fact. In essence, it announced to the world: here is a value packaged offer that is worth $125 but you only pay $85 for it. So the $40 savings is yours.

Why would a business provide added value to the customer for a reduced price, particularly since there would be added costs such as marketing and advertising associated to create the offer and take it to market? Even if this offer were successful, I suspect the restaurant was challenged to earn a profit margin commensurate with the value provided.

In pricing bundled offers it's not simply a matter of adding up the components of the offer and discounting their total cost, but rather of price positioning the offer in relation to the competition.

In this example, the restaurant would have been wise to first consider what sort of offer would effectively compete with their package. They mistakenly held to the incorrect notion that the customer needed the added incentive of a substantial discount to favorably respond to an already excellent offer.

The Be Different approach would have been to price position the offer in relation to another hockey-night-out alternative, the Canucks, for example, and establish it as a premium to the total individual offer components. It might have been more appropriate to price the offer at $150, a bargain compared to the cost of a Canuck's hockey night out, and take the additional $25 contribution to recover the marketing investment.

Bundling up to get lower prices just doesn't cut it.

Here is another example of a bundle offered by a financial institution that advertised customer rewards for signing up to a bigger bundle. The ad invited you to choose the bundle 'that works for you — the more you 'bundle up' the better the pricing on your mortgage.' In addition you received other services. Here's how it worked:

- Bundle #1 – 5.62% Mortgage + Day-to-day Banking

- Bundle #2 – 5.59% Mortgage + New Investment or Deposit

- Bundle #3 – 5.56% Mortgage + Both of the Above

Now, there were a number of terms and conditions that applied which actually restricted the open selling of the bundles, but this is the essence of what they were offering. Again, this exhibits the common bundling theme by dangling lower prices, mortgage rates in this case, for bundles with more capabilities; bundling up to get lower prices is simply not, in my opinion, an effective strategy.

As a third example, the Canadian Imperial Bank of Commerce (CIBC) mentioned earlier in the book is a financial institution trying to develop an *only* statement related to its latest credit card product. It took the only Infinite Card a step further and created a packaged offer around it. Let's review its actions here, as there are some interesting issues relating to both the offer itself and how they have chosen to price-position it. Recall their *only* statement:

'The *only* Infinite Card made from pure gold.'

The offer contains these elements:

- '1.5 air miles for every dollar spent on gas, groceries and drugstores

- Free extended privileges at select hotels and restaurants

- Prestige of travel concierge service, free

- Peace of mind of 15-day travel medical insurance, free'

So, buy its card and the value you receive consists of airline miles when you purchase specific goods and services, special privileges at certain hotels and restaurants (no details however to judge the value provided), travel concierge service (again no details) and medical travel insurance which they at least say it is for fifteen days. In concept, it is an approach which, with a bit more work, could actually be quite good, except for the 'free' references to the non-financial components of the offer. All of the value that CIBC is adding to its fundamental banking product, the card, is free. The message I get from their strategy is, once again, get more value and pay less.

It is a common strategy for banks to offer value-added bundles to the market at discounted prices. At face value, they do it to increase the loyalty of their existing customer base, for without the bundles, customers would move to another financial provider. However, since they all seem to be taking a similar approach, how can any one of the bundles increase customer loyalty?

The CIBC example is of particular concern to me as they are adding non-financial products to their bundle and apparently choosing to underwrite the costs. The business case for this decision might make sense based on the economics of customer card retention, but if you believed, as I do, that the nature of this bundle isn't really unique and that it can be copied by others, any added provisioning costs are coming out of the margin earned on the card product itself. Why would you do it?

To repeat: you need to think of your offer as a premium value offering that should command a premium price. Remember, if you have done your homework on needs plus secrets and have created a relevant and compelling set of customer values you should have no problem in getting a premium price for it.

6. Brand the offer

Branding is very much a part of Being Different. If you take the bundling world approach and make the offer brand bundle-centric like the Telecom bundle or home finance bundles, for example, you are missing the holistic offer concept and an enormous opportunity to set your organization apart from your competitors. Through holistic offers you are creating additional value for your customers, so your brand should reflect this new innovative value package. This is a chance to communicate something completely new and different from anyone else out there. It is also an opportunity to be recognized as an innovator, constantly bringing new products to the market. Take advantage of the opportunity and get credit for it.

Holistic offers provide additional value; create a Be Different brand to reflect it.

In determining the brand for your offer, be guided by the value proposition that you have created. In our financial services example, this was our *only* statement:

'We are the only ones that offer a package of personal services that enable you to effectively manage your world. We make it easy for you to work hard and play hard.'

The high level attributes of the brand relate to personal services and managing your world to remove the stress and hassle in your life. If we choose these as the value drivers we have a number of potential brands that we could consider.

- *Your World* managed for you by your financial institution

- *The Most Personal Service Package* from your financial institution

To support the brand, obviously you will have substantial collateral material that not only discusses the offer's capabilities, but also presents the business partnerships you have assembled to deliver the compelling value to the customer. This will establish your organization as a leader in marketing and one that is committed to serving customers in an ever meaningful way.

A strategic pause doesn't constitute incompetence; it exhibits understanding of brilliant implementation.

7. Go to market

Go-to-market planning must consider:

- Sales channels

- Profitability objectives

- Sales targets and timelines

- Operational procedures and processes

- Partner performance plans

- Employee training

- Customer communications

- Employee communications to explain the offer, the strategy behind it, the business partners that have been developed and the results expected.

Don't launch too early. I have seen excellent marketing programs without adequate preparation fail due to a desire to get to market quickly. Flawed implementation will diminish the value you claim to provide. Wait until your employees tell you they feel competent to do this. A strategic pause doesn't constitute incompetence; rather, it exhibits understanding of brilliant implementation.

At TELUS, we developed our own *campaign management* discipline for taking offers to market. This process consisted of establishing integrated quarterly campaign plans complete with a calendar showing the timing and fit of each marketing program in the campaign. The results of each campaign were monitored weekly, monthly and quarterly in order to initiate any corrective action that was required due to unexpected execution issues — planning on the run in action.

8. Learn and tweak

The final step under the ask-the-customer method of creating holistic offers relates to what you do when your offer is in the market. In Section Two I discussed the notions of being anal about execution and planning on the run. Apply these principles here and link the two ideas. Effective execution focus means that you are open and thirsty to understand how the offer is performing: what is working, what is not and what you need to do to get things back on track.

Campaign management is a disciplined approach to taking holistic offers to market.

Here are some questions you should ask yourself during the implementation phase.

- Is the value proposition resonating with the customer?

- Is it causing a competitive response?

- Is the pricing plan working?

- Are the operating procedures working?

- Was the training effective?

- What can employees tell us? What are their experiences?

- Are there any business partner relationship issues that need to be addressed?

- Is the advertising plan meeting its objectives? Are sales targets being achieved?

With this type of feedback information, be prepared to tweak things to produce better overall results. Remember, it is very unlikely that you will get it right the first time, due to unforeseen events and the fact that people are involved in the implementation process and they are not perfect. So be prepared and open to making changes to move toward flawless execution; exceeding your overall targets will be more within your reach.

Be prepared to tweak things to improve your offer performance. You're unlikely to get it right the first time.

QUICK HITS

■ Here are the ten steps in building the *ask the customer* offer process:

1. Segment your customer base using the appropriate segmentation method to determine which customer groups present the greatest value to you.

2. Make a customer attributes map using the needs-plus-secrets information that you have discovered about the target customers.

3. Group this customer information into a number of value components that easily communicate the value you are providing.

4. Create a unique value proposition defining the benefits you intend to provide. Remember you need to position yourself as the only organization delivering this value.

5. Define the capabilities needed to deliver your value proposition. Capabilities are not only products and services that you provide, but also those provided by other organizations.

6. Integrate the capabilities into a cohesive expression of value for the customer. This is where the individual product and service components must come together synergistically and be provided in a way that is seamless to the customer.

7. Price the offer. The guiding principle is to charge premium prices for the greater value that you bring the customer; price discounting for bundles doesn't cut it.

8. Brand your offer. Create something new. Be guided by your value proposition.

9. Go to market. Consider developing a campaign management process that takes a variety of offers to your targeted customers on a regularly scheduled basis. And tenaciously measure the sales results.

10. Learn and tweak. Build a feedback loop into your process to take advantage of the field experience you get from seeing how your offer performs in the market.

Offer Creation Method #2 — Understanding Customer Behavior

The second method of building a holistic offer uses customer product and services behavior data to define natural groups of products and services that can be sold together. In addition, you can go further to combine your own products and services with products and services provided by other organizations. For example, you could learn that a customer group buys high speed Internet service and a wireless modem from you at the same time; from customer secrets you learn that the group also upgrades its computers which you can source from one of your partners.

Another method uses customer product and services behavior to define natural groups of products and services that can be sold together.

A *natural product group* consists of a number of products that can be attached or put together in a way that produces a common benefit or value theme for the targeted customers. The process usually starts with defining an *anchor product* and then attaching other products and services, yours and others, to it, forming a natural product group. This is a very practical approach but it requires diligent work to choose products and services that imply a unique value proposition based on their common value theme.

The first example involves a financial institution that has decided to build an offer around its mortgage product. This is the process:

1. Define the mortgage product as the anchor.

2. Add line of credit and wealth management services (internal capabilities).

3. Add home insurance and home maintenance services (external capabilities).

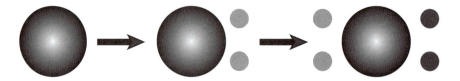

What might the value proposition for this offer be? In this case, the product capabilities are organized around a theme of managing your home and enhancing your life and I think both dimensions to the offer are highly synergistic. From this theme the value proposition could be described as 'We make it easy for you to access resources you need to enjoy your home and enhance your life.' Take this a step further and create a unique brand for the offer: 'Your Own Home and Life Plan,' using the value proposition as the tag line.

In the second example, a telecommunications company has decided to create an offer built around their high speed Internet service.

1. Define high speed Internet as the anchor.

2. Add voice-over IP and mobility services (internal capabilities).

3. Add a laptop computer, a wireless modem and a PDA (external capabilities).

The product capability theme could be 'Unleash the power of the Internet anytime, anywhere,' as clearly the products chosen allow you to use the Internet anywhere in your home via wireless modem, and outside of your home on laptop computer and PDA. In addition, mobility devices allow for on-the-move Internet access, enabling both voice calls and e-mail communication. The value proposition for the offer could be: 'The Internet is for you anywhere and anytime' and the brand could be 'Your Personal Internet Suite brought to you by...'

I read about an offer from Alaska Airlines targeting families who were interested in going to Disneyland. The package was branded Kids Fly Free and contained the following elements:

• Round-trip air travel between Vancouver and Los Angeles for one adult and one child

• Accommodation for four nights

• Free child's meal with the purchase of an adult meal

- Five-day Disneyland Resort Park Hopper ticket for one child and one adult for the price of a three-day ticket

- 1,500 Alaska Airlines bonus miles per person in addition to the regular miles earned from the flight when booked on line at alaskaair.com

Again, this is a productive approach by Alaska Airlines who are adding the Disneyland experience oriented to children to their basic flight product. Disneyland really is a kids-of-all-ages' experience and designing the value of the offer to make it easier for parents to take their kids there makes a lot of sense.

As an aside, I'm less impressed with the pricing structure of the offer. There are numerous references to price discounting ('Kids Fly Free', free child's meal with the purchase of an adult meal, five-day Disneyland ticket for the price of a three-day one) which may indicate the company is not in the premium pricing mode.

This is the approach they used:

1. Select air transportation to L.A. as the anchor product.

2. Add free child fare and 1,500 bonus points (internal capabilities).

3. Add hotel and Disneyland tickets (external capabilities).

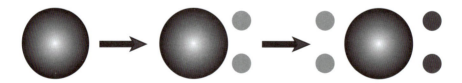

Our discussion so far suggests that customer purchasing behavior should govern the characteristics of the holistic offer. A spin on this approach would be to use good old-fashioned marketing intuition rather than explicit behavioral data to select the products and services that could be put together to form a natural product group. I have seen this work, but only when a strong synergistic value proposition is created that resonates strongly with customers.

You don't always need detailed and rigorous analysis to come up with a winning offer, although in the long run you will win more often if you do your homework. If your gut tells you that two of your products represent a natural product group and you are able to develop a strong value proposition for it, then try it, track it and trash it if it doesn't work. Or pat yourself on the back if it does.

If your gut tells you that two of your products represent a natural product group and you are able to develop a strong value proposition for it, then try it, track it and trash it if it doesn't work. Or pat yourself on the back if it does.

Apple is a great example of a company that has created the ability to transform their anchor product into a broad range of experience-based holistic offers. With their focus on *"an App for this and an App for that"* they have created the ability to mass customize numerous value-based Offers to satisfy the divergent needs of their customer base. With over ninety thousand specific Apps developed for their iPhone, people are able to access a broad range of experiences from *Wine Ph. D* for wine lovers to *Style.com* for the fashionistas.

■ Here is the ten-step *understanding customer behavior* offer building process. Note that the latter steps are common to the *ask the customer* process.

1. Segment your customer base using behavior information and any predictive modeling that will give you insights into, first, which segments present the greatest value to you and second, which product groups are popular choices for each segment.

2. Determine the anchor product or service that represents the nucleus of the offer.

3. Define the secondary products and services that work well with the anchor product to complete the offer. These can be products or services that you provide; they can also be products and services of other organizations.

4. Develop a common value theme for the offer that ties all of the individual products and services together.

5. Create the unique value proposition for the offer. The offer is not equal to the sum of its parts. It is more.

6. Integrate the products and services through a process that is seamless from the customer's perspective.

7. Price the offer. Remember, adding value should command premium pricing; discounting reduces margins and communicates lower value.

8. Brand the offer. Be bold and creative. You are creating something new; brand it so.

9. Go to market and consider acquiring campaign management competencies to plan and control the process.

10. Learn and tweak. Plan on the run.

Chapter Twenty-Eight

Customerized Marketing Operating Model

We have discussed a number of Be Different ideas that will *customerize* your marketing competencies:

- Customer learning

- Customer secrets

- Holistic offer

- Unique value proposition

- Creative brands

- Go-to-market campaigns

The marketing operating model orchestrates the activities necessary to execute offers brilliantly.

To yield the maximum value from these ideas you need to construct an operating model that defines how the ideas relate to each other in process terms. Building an operating model has at least two benefits: first it enables everyone in the organization to see the big picture in terms of how everything fits together, and then it lays out the framework for tracking and measuring the effectiveness of your marketing programs.

The operating model we built at TELUS involved four components, an approach not for larger companies only; smaller organizations can approach the challenge with the same logic.

- Understanding the customer – gathering as much information as you can about the customer through segmentation, customer research and behavior analysis. Lifetime value assessment was also included

- Creating customer value – constructing a unique value proposition, creating the offer and integrating the capabilities required to deliver the offer

- Delivering customer value – the go-to-market phase: launching offers through quarterly campaigns, targeting the intended customer, monitoring results and taking corrective action based on market response

- Maximizing customer value – creating the optimum value for both the customer and the company

Customerized Marketing Operating Model

Understand the Customer +	Create Customer Value +	Deliver Value
• Needs plus secrets	• Unique value proposition	• Quarterly plan
• Customer behavior	• Offer creation	• Target the individual
• Current value	• Capabilities & integration	• Manage the investment
• Potential value		• Launch offers
• Investment risk		• Manage results

Maximize Customer Value

QUICK HITS

■ Construct a marketing operating model to integrate the Be Different marketing ideas.

■ Use it to communicate to your organization the new marketing process and how the company can support your efforts.

■ Develop a measurement system to determine the return on your marketing investment.

Chapter Twenty-Nine

No IT Support, No BE DiFFERENT Marketing

How do you execute this customerized marketing operating model? You can't stop with the notion that an operations process needs to be developed to deliver the Be Different marketing capabilities. You need to move on and create the ability to deliver them.

There could be numerous approaches to this, depending on the size of your organization and the complexities of the customer markets you intend to serve. For example, if you have a small business with a few customer groups you probably will want to employ a simple process using manual methods and minimize the requirement for information technology investment. On the other hand, if your business is larger and you have a number of complex customer segments, a more sophisticated solution might be appropriate.

Database marketing (DBM) is a proven, effective tool in supporting the Be Different marketing efforts of organizations. We implemented it at TELUS, but it is appropriate for organizations of all sizes due to the generic actions needed to implement it. If you have a small business, for example, consider DBM as a menu of things that you need to do in whatever way makes sense to you.

DBM offers the following Be Different benefits:

- Understanding which customers and prospects are the most valuable today and are likely to be in the future

- Delivering highly targeted offers, across multiple sales channels

- Strengthening customer loyalty by delivering what customers want in the manner they want it

- Increasing the profitability of the business

Database marketing is an effective tool to implement your operating model making offer creation a reality.

DBM is an excellent approach, but requires some IT investment to bring it to life and deliver the benefits to an organization with a large number of customers. It provides marketers with the ability to segment markets and identify the attractive customers to target, creates repositories of customer needs plus secrets and develops the analysis/decision-making tools required to create the right offers for the right customers.

To develop competence in database marketing start with a definition of the key deliverables you expect from it:

To enable customer learning:

- Ask-the-customer data

- Customer behavior profiles

- Customer segmentation

- Predictive models

- Customer profitability

- Customer churn analysis – customer profitability is directly related to how frequently customers come and go

- Investment decision tools – which customers to invest in? Which offer produces the optimum return on investment made?

To support effective campaign management:

- Quarterly campaign sizing and prioritization – how many offers should be included in each campaign? How should the offers be prioritized based on customer importance, return on investment and competitive pressures?

- Test cell design – campaigns are tested before launching to the total target customer group. How should the test cell look for the required level of confidence from the full campaign target?

- Customer campaign lists

- Campaign tracking and reporting – did the campaign hit its targets?

The IT people should be able to look at the DBM components and easily define what IT capability needs to be developed.

Database Marketing Components

Customer Learning

Customer research
Behavior tracking
Customer Profitability
Credit history
Customer churn
Current value
Offer profitability
Customer revenue
Offer revenue tracking

Decision Tools

Predictive tools
Segmentation
Campaign priorities
Customer potential value

Execution and Tracking

Campaign management
Relationship building – Share of customer
Tracking & measurement
Learn-and-tweak discipline

With these expectations in mind, the next step at TELUS was to define the various components that would be required in the DBM system, as shown in the figure above. We defined the precise activities to be followed in order to inform the development of the IT capability required. In other words, the IT people needed to be able to look at the DBM components and easily define what IT capability needed to be developed. If you have decided not to adopt an IT development process, at least the DBM components will guide you in terms of the things you need to do in whatever method you choose to support your Be Different marketing operations model.

The third step was to meet with IT to initiate the development process. We outlined our database marketing expectations and the overall strategy driving it. Although they were accountable to create the IT tools necessary to get the functionality we needed, we chose to provide them with some overall guidance in terms of marketing's needs:

- We needed to see an *IT roadmap* that would ensure our needs were met, complete with the specific tools provided and when they would be available.

- We needed an *IT toolbox* that was easy to use for end-user marketing analysts and managers. In addition, the toolbox would have to be open-ended and flexible enough to satisfy any new specialized applications that might arise.

In many organizations, marketing is a second cousin to other departments when it comes to IT investment. This needs to change if you want to Be Different.

- We had specific response times in mind when there were IT service issues affecting our ability to get things done. We specified our service level expectations and did our best to balance them with IT's capability to meet them.

- Finally, we asked that the system be built as an Internet portal which could be accessed by our marketing folks anytime and from anywhere.

We realized that our database marketing vision at TELUS was a significant undertaking. As you know, in many organizations marketing has been a second cousin to other departments when it comes to IT investment. I have witnessed, for example, other departments such as engineering and operations get top priority for IT resources, leaving marketing and sales with only residual funds for their budgetary needs. Putting a priority on marketing was a watershed experience for my colleagues and me, signaling to the organization at large that customer-inspired marketing activity was a fundamental part of the company's strategic future.

To reinforce the following specific points:

Customer Learning – Data warehouses need to be developed and populated not only with product and service use behavior information about a customer, but also with needs-plus-secrets information gathered from your customer contact points. Capturing this open-format type of information is a challenge, but CRM technologies can do it for you.

Product-centric accounting systems cannot deliver offer-centric information without major re-design.

Revenue Tracking by Offer – Most companies track revenue by product. Moving to offers which have a number of products becomes an interesting challenge. I recall one conversation I had with our CFO about this and his view was 'We will need to completely redesign all of our accounting systems to get the information needed.' It's true, product-centric accounting systems simply cannot deliver offer-centric information without major re-design.

Offer Profitability – Product profitability in organizations generally is a challenge due to the inability to identify all the causal costs attributable to a particular product and also to the need to allocate common costs of the organization across the product portfolio. Offer profitability, given that it consists of a number of product capabilities, is even more of a challenge, particularly if you decide to introduce a product or service component from another organization. How do you identify all of the causal costs for an offer? How do you capture them on an ongoing basis and match them with the corresponding revenue stream?

Customer Profitability – If you go to the trouble of building your strategy to select a customer group to serve, you had better know whether you made the right decision. Revenue by customer is an important indicator of the right customer choice, but you also need to look at the bottom line that each customer gives your organization through the transactions with you.

QUICK HITS

- Once you have developed your marketing operations model, you need to determine how to make it work. Smaller businesses require simpler systems to do this; larger organizations require substantial IT support.

- Attracting appropriate IT resources requires that you develop a detailed view of the marketing capabilities for which you are looking. If you cannot communicate the detailed functionality that you need, it will be difficult for the IT folks to be able to respond to you.

- Database Marketing (DBM) is a discipline that provides a framework to define precisely what functionality is needed.

- DBM should be developed as a core competency of your organization; it requires the following steps:

  - Create your customized operations model: what process do you need to deliver your Be Different marketing capabilities?

  - Set your database marketing expectations: what are you trying to achieve to execute your operations process?

- Develop your own database marketing model with the required components. This will be the translator between your marketing expectations and the Information Technology folks in terms of the capabilities they must create for you.

- Create the IT infrastructure and specific tools that will deliver your database model.

- Work closely with IT to ensure that they clearly understand what you need and that you understand their ability to deliver.

If you are a smaller business you can still follow the above process. It will simply require less IT sophistication to deliver the functionality you need.

Chapter Thirty

Restructure to the Customer

A *customerized* organization adds a second organizational dimension to your marketing efforts. Most marketing organizations have marketers that focus on products and services; a customerized one also has teams that are responsible for groups of customers. In this sense, the Be Different marketing organization has a matrix style in which both a product and a customer focus co-exist to optimize the organization's overall performance.

Customer Marketing + Product Marketing = The Be Different Marketing Team

I am not suggesting that product teams are no longer needed and that you can only be successful with customer oriented teams. On the contrary, I think the product focus must continue to play a strong marketing role in any organization, but not the only role. Organizations that are serious about making the change to Be Different have structures that represent these two types of marketing: product marketing and customer marketing. Here's a quick overview of the responsibilities of each.

Customer Marketing: The customer marketing teams are generally organized around key customer segments the organization has chosen to serve through the strategy building exercise. They are accountable for any activity that is required to successfully take an offer to market, including providing direction to the product marketing teams to ensure that appropriate product capabilities are developed for their customer segment.

Here are some specific responsibilities of the customer teams:

- Offer creation and pricing

- Customer share and revenue

- Customer growth planning

- Channel management

- Channel incentives

- Customer profitability

- Customer communications

Customerized marketing requires product managers to support their customer marketing counterparts.

Product Marketing: The product marketing team is accountable for providing support to customer marketing. In this sense, they are responsible for developing the product capabilities that customer marketing requires to create offers for their chosen customer segment.

Here are some detailed responsibilities:

- Product pricing guidelines. The final decision on pricing an offer, however, rests with the customer marketing teams

- Outside product supplier relationships

- Product profitability

- New offer capabilities

- Product development

- Managing market share for products

- Technology adoption

During my tenure with BC Telecom, I established both organizations in the customer facing marketing division. Reporting to me as the VP Marketing and Sales were:

- Director — Customer Marketing

- Director — Product Marketing

- Director — Sales

The customer marketing team had the following functional areas:

- Consumer market leader

- Business market leader

- Advertising

- Market research and competitive intelligence

- Database marketing

- Campaign management

- Channel strategy and planning

- Financial forecasting and reporting

Customer marketing creates a cultural shock for product management, the sole engine driving marketing efforts up to this time.

The product managers were faced with the fact that not only was there now another marketing team that assumed some of their previous responsibilities — channel management and customer communications, for example — their role was now more of a supportive one to this new group.

The transition from being the prime drivers of all marketing activity to a supportive role with less responsibility was a difficult one for many product managers, and required very clear and constant communication for each group. And it required patience, as the expected results from the added customer dimension were not realized overnight.

QUICK HITS

- Organizational structure should always be viewed as the means to achieve your Be Different marketing operations process. If resources are not allocated and applied in a manner that is consistent with your new process, you won't achieve your desired outcome.

- The marketing organization should be set up with two disciplines: product marketing and customer marketing.

- Customer managers are responsible for all offers to the customer segment for which they are responsible.

- Product managers are responsible for their assigned product across all customer segments.

Chapter Thirty-One

Customer Share: The New Success Measure

Traditional marketing organizations use market share as a key measurement to determine market success. Market share typically measures the percentage of a particular market segment held by a product or service across all addressable customers and is used primarily by product focused organizations.

For example, the market share for a high speed Internet service could be 60% of the addressable residential market, that is, the portion of the market where high speed Internet is technically available in any given area. This measurement would interest the product manager for high speed Internet services. It would certainly drive marketing programs to increase the market share of the service in terms of not only taking a share of the competition, but also in capturing a higher proportion of any new market growth.

To Be Different, though, this measurement simply doesn't go far enough.

Customer share, on the other hand, is a key measure of success used by a customerized organization. Customer share is sometimes referred to as share of wallet. Information technology measures the share of a customer's total spending in one of your business sectors across all of your business services. For example, if your organization has a 20% share of residential Telecom users in Greater Vancouver, then for every $100 these customers spend on Telecom services you are getting $20 from all of the telecom services you provide, such as Internet, mobility, long distance and local services.

Be Different marketing uses customer share as the prime performance measure. Market share is relevant but is in the number two position.

This measure is the more relevant one for businesses choosing customer groups to serve and wanting to understand how effectively they are penetrating these groups with their entire set of offerings. The implications for marketing program development are clear, using customer share measure. In this case, holding only 20% should drive an aggressive growth strategy across a number of offers to increase the percentage of total telecom business. I have always characterized a low customer share position as having a tremendous growth opportunity!

I am not suggesting that market share is a worthless measurement or that it should be eliminated in favor of customer share. To qualify as a customerized marketing organization, however, customer share should be adopted as the key tool and should be used in addition to a market share view of your products and services. Furthermore, I would suggest that, over time, measuring customer share needs to take a more predominant role as an indicator of Be Different market success.

QUICK HITS

- Customer share is the measurement aligned with the Be Different marketing approach for selecting the highest value groups of customers that you intend to serve, and then penetrating each group with as many offers as possible.

- Think about customer share as the percentage of a customer's business that you have in your particular business category. It will tell you how effective you have been in comparison with your competition. A 10% customer share means you have a lot of work to do; 90% customer share means look out! Your competitors are watching.

- Set customer share objectives for your targeted customer groups consistent with your overall strategic game plan. They should reflect HOW BIG you want to be and should drive holistic offer development activity. For example, objectives to double customer share might require a significant budget increase to your customer marketing efforts; you need to be prepared to make it.

- A low share position = a tremendous growth opportunity.

185

Chapter Thirty-Two

Champion the BE DiFFERENT Profit Equation

The traditional profit equation that organizations use leaves little opportunity to Be Different and poses significant survival risk. Marketing, as the owner of offer profitability, needs to demonstrate strong leadership to introduce a new approach.

Consider the basic economics equation, Profit = Revenue – Cost. It seems fairly straightforward. The inputs to the equation, independent variables, are revenue, what the market is willing to pay you for the goods and services you provide, and the cost you incur in taking those goods and services to market. Profit, the dependent variable, is what remains after subtracting costs from revenues. At the product or service level, however, I have rarely seen the actual profit generated turn out to be what the equation predicted.

The traditional profit equation that organizations use leaves little opportunity to Be Different and poses significant survival risk.

The most common problem is that actual profits are below profit objectives. Have you seen this as well? Why do you suppose this happens? We don't estimate revenue accurately and/or we underestimate the costs involved. In any event, the result is that the shareholder or business owner bears the loss. And worse than that, the risk of 'being dead' just went up another notch.

I think the equation is all wrong. There is a way, however, to achieve desired profit levels and immunize your organization against early mortality. Consider this formula:

Cost = Revenue – Profit

In this paradigm, both revenue and profit are inputs to the cost equation as opposed to revenue and cost being inputs to the profit equation. This is not sleight of hand. The market claims its impact, customers pay us revenue and investors get their fair share. Profits are taken first from the revenue stream; what is left over is the cost that you can afford to operate the business. In other words, in this system, cost ends up being the dependent variable and it varies directly with the inputs of revenue and profit.

The Be Different profit equation:
Cost = Revenue – Profit

If, for example, you calculated that you would generate $100 revenue from offer X, and the margin objectives for this were 40%, the cost target your organization would face is $60. If you could take the offer to market and sustain it for $60 or less, then go ahead and introduce it. If on the other hand your organization feels that this offer cannot be supplied at the $60 level, you really have only two choices:

1. Don't introduce the offer, or

2. Introduce it and get less than objective returns from it. In other words, take it out of the investor's/owner's wallet.

Regardless of the reason, if you decide to introduce the offer, ensure that you assign responsibility and accountability for the cost targets to those key managers in the organization responsible for the various cost elements. And, to make it matter for them, include this in their performance plan.

It is necessary to track both cost and revenue results. Likely they will not perform as predicted. There are a number of actions you can take depending on the nature of the variance. I am assuming that the investor's return will be protected, and that allowing margins to shrink is simply not an option.

- If revenue is over target, and costs are within target limits, *delight your investor/owner* with excess profit. This will offset any underperformance from other offers.

- If revenue is over target, and costs are above objective, reduce costs to pass the excess benefits to the investor. It is extremely important to establish the discipline of achieving cost targets, even though you may be hitting margin objectives on the back of healthy revenues.

- If revenue is under target, as are costs, adjust cost targets to maintain margins.

- If revenue is below target and costs are above limits, adjust cost targets to achieve margin objectives.

- Last, but certainly not least, if margins are suffering from higher costs than anticipated, the marketer should also be looking for opportunities to increase revenue by adding value to the service and charging a higher price. As long as you have a customer willing to pay more for greater benefits and the price exceeds the cost of delivering it, this option provides a way to get back on the margin track.

This approach demands that marketing groups lead implementation in an organization. They are responsible for understanding the nature of customer demand and developing prices accordingly. They own the revenue stream. Furthermore, since most organizations hold marketing groups accountable for product profitability, they are best able to lead the organization to develop cost targets and monitor them to ensure they are attained.

Here is a step-by-step approach to implement the Cost = Revenue – Profit method.

1. Determine the price level that customers are willing to pay for the offer.

2. Develop a revenue projection based on expected demand.

3. Establish the profitability objectives for the offer, and calculate the margin required from the anticipated revenue.

4. Determine the total cost objective for the offer using the Cost = Revenue – Profit formula.

5. Identify the various cost components that are at play in the supply of the offer, sales, marketing, billing, etc.

6. Weight each cost component in terms of the percentage of total cost it contributes. For example, sales might represent 20% of the total cost; advertising, 10%.

7. Set cost targets for each cost component.

8. Ask the various internal organizations that manage each of these costs whether or not they can meet their cost targets.

If the answer is yes, proceed to market. If no, look for alternate ways to introduce the offer and satisfy cost objectives, or get approval to go to market at below target margin levels, or don't take the offer to market.

In my view the long term challenge is to recruit people with the skills and competencies necessary to reinvent supply systems in order to deliver the future cost targets of the business. I realize that separate systems can't be developed for each and every offer an organization supplies. However, supply platforms can be developed to best meet the needs of groups of offers at expected market prices. What offers do you think will be required over the next five years? What price levels do you think the marketplace will support? What margin expectations will your business demand? What supply costs are implied? What supply infrastructure can be adopted to meet 80% of the implied costs? These are all salient questions that must be answered to get to the Cost = Revenue – Profit, Be Different world.

■ The traditional Profit = Revenue – Cost formula creates dysfunctional behavior; the owner/shareholder always seems to get stuck when costs are higher than plan and revenues are lower than plan.

■ The Be Different formula Cost = Revenue – Profit places cost in a box determined by what the market will give you and what the owners of the business expect.

■ The Be Different approach is revenue/profit-driven costing, not revenue/cost-driven profitability.

Chapter Thirty-Three

Stick the Competition Where It Belongs

The classic term used to describe the competitive landscape in a business is 'barriers to competitive entry'. When developing a marketing strategy we often refer to barriers to competitive entry as an assessment of the relative success we might enjoy due to the difficulty or ease that competitors could experience in entering our target markets.

Your main concern should be customers leaving, rather than competitors entering.

Barriers to entry include:

- Technology. You have a head start with a unique technology that will not likely be matched for some time.

- Regulation. There are regulatory rules and policies that prevent others from entering your market under the same terms and conditions that you now enjoy. Re-read Section One.

- Investment. You have made significant financial investments to achieve your current market position and others would not likely be prepared to invest as heavily to challenge you.

- Brand. You have substantial equity in your brand, making it difficult for others to successfully compete with you.

In one way, thinking about your competitive position from the point of view of barriers does have benefits. It does give you a perspective on how easily you might lose your position in the market to someone else. And with this knowledge you can, as part of your marketing strategy, perhaps erect barriers or strengthen any existing ones.

It is this perspective that has always concerned me. We focus heavily on determining what has to be done in order to prevent others from taking business from us, as opposed to figuring out what we need to do to prevent our customers from leaving. Why devote significant resources to issues over which we have little control when there is an opportunity to spend our time on more controllable issues?

What are you doing to erect barriers to customer exit, on actions to build customer loyalty?

I maintain we should be spending more time determining what can be done to create customer stickiness or *barriers to customer exit*, what we can do to build customer loyalty. Do what is necessary to prevent your competitors from encroaching on your turf but also start spending as much or more time doing things to keep your customers from leaving. Have the customer drive your strategy more than the competition.

I believe we need a more balanced approach: observe the competition, but act for the customer. Continue to be aware of your competitors and their specific strategies, but put plans and programs in place to keep customers from leaving you.

QUICK HITS

■ Be Different organizations think more about creating barriers to customer exit than erecting barriers to competitive entry.

■ You really do have more control over preventing customers from leaving you than you do over keeping the competition out. So deal with what you can control.

■ Creating barriers to customer exit results in organizational behavior focused on the customer and looking for ways to increase customer loyalty.

■ Be aware of what your competitors are doing, but make sure that your actions are targeted to getting customers to stay with you in the face of competitive activity as opposed to spending all of your time trying to keep competitors from your door.

■ Observe the competition and act for the customer.

SECTION THREE LEARNING POINTS

✓ In order to Be Different, organizations need to morph to customerized marketing and go beyond Marketing 101.

✓ *Customerization* involves a fundamental shift in emphasis from focusing on products that satisfy the needs of broad market segments to creating holistic offers that are based on the requirements of smaller customer groups.

✓ *Customer learning* is the continuous process of gathering information on customers in a manner that will drive Be Different marketing programs.

✓ There are two ways to implement customer learning: *asking the customer* and *understanding customer behavior*.

Asking the customer supplements traditional market research methods with customer information gathered from many customer contact points in an organization. Treat a customer contact as a moment of strategic opportunity.

Understanding customer behavior involves developing customer information through tracking and analyzing the way in which customers interact with your organization and how they use your products and services.

✓ Customer learning involves a different approach to segmenting your market. Unlike mass marketing, it uses many segmentation variables to define many small segments to get a deep understanding of the individuals in each segment. In a group of one hundred customers you know more about each of them than if you had a group of a thousand. Marketers, keep on segmenting!

✓ Customer learning must be instituted throughout your organization to make getting close to the customer a continuous process; this should be a core competency of your business and a key descriptor of your culture.

- ✓ Discover *customer secrets* in addition to traditional customer needs. Through relationship building, develop intimate knowledge of each of your customers and small customer segments as the underpinning of your Be Different strategy. Ensure that this knowledge drives marketing development activities as well as sales and service.

- ✓ There are two practical approaches to creating *holistic offers* depending on the customer learning method you choose: asking the customer and understanding customer behavior. Decide which method works for your organization but remember that, to be successful in either case, you need to develop a compelling and unique value proposition that resonates with your target customers.

- ✓ A holistic offer is not a bundle. Price it at a premium consistent with the value provided. Do not price discount.

- ✓ In order to implement the portfolio of Be Different marketing ideas, you need an operating model and process that defines the relationships between ideas and provides a basis for measuring marketing effectiveness.

- ✓ Build a Database Marketing (DBM) capability in your organization based on your operating model. Use DBM as the vehicle to define and communicate your marketing requirements to the IT people. Remember, small organizations can use DBM principles even though it might be inappropriate to make substantial IT investments.

- ✓ Reorganize your marketing department so that the customer gets a prominent place. Keep your product marketing teams but change their role to support the new *customer marketing* organization.

- ✓ As the key measurement of success for the Be Different marketing organization, measure *customer share* or share of wallet. The traditional market share measurement is still relevant but it is not characteristic of Being Different.

✓ Profits are always scarce. Be Different and adopt the *Cost = Revenue – Profit* paradigm for managing your marketing returns on investment.

✓ Put the competition in its place. Observe what they are up to and learn as much as you can about each of them, but don't get mesmerized by barriers to entry. Look for ways to keep customers from leaving you rather than just considering ways to keep competitors out. Aggressively act for customers, enhancing their loyalty and creating *barriers to customer exit.*

✓ Here is a summary of the difference between traditional marketing concepts and the customerized approach.

Marketing 101	Customerized Marketing
Market research	Customer learning
A few customer segments	Many segments
General customer knowledge	Specific knowledge of a customer in the segment
Average customer	Unique customer
Customer needs	Customer needs + secrets
Products and services	Holistic offers
Product marketing	Customer marketing
Profit = Revenue – cost	Cost = Revenue – profit
Market share	Customer share
Barriers to competitive entry	Barriers to customer exit

Section Four

BE DiFFERENT Serving Customers

Chapter Thirty-Four

Serve Customers, Don't Provide Customer Service

The fourth aspect of an organization that can be leveraged to Be Different is what has been traditionally referred to as customer service. I prefer the term serving customers, however, as it describes the essence of what is required to Be Different from a service perspective.

The term customer service has been used by most organizations to describe what the company has decided to do to service the customer after the sale has been made. So, servicing the customer has taken on several characteristics:

- It essentially represents what the company decides to provide or push to the customer in after-sale engagement.

- It is usually articulated by the organization as a policy or portfolio of rules and procedures that must be followed by all employees, particularly those having direct contact with customers.

- It usually involves similar treatment of all customers regardless of their individual characteristics and without discrimination.

- The level of servicing provided is strongly influenced by the level of cost the organization is prepared to incur.

Serving the customer places the customer — *not the company* — in the control position.

- The company is responding to the service expectations of customers rather than deciding in advance what they are prepared to provide to them. It is a 'customer pull' model, where service policy is engineered from the customer's viewpoint.

- Service policy is customer inspired but customer-contact employees are empowered to break the rules, when necessary, to accommodate a legitimate customer concern.

- Service philosophy is guided by the customerized notion that each customer is unique, and that providing varying levels of service is appropriate to achieving a consistent level of customer satisfaction.

Servicing the customer represents what the company decides to provide the customer. Serving the customer places the customer in the control position.

- The level of cost that the organization incurs in serving customers is treated as an investment in creating customer value rather than simply as an operating cost. Cost is important, but service decisions are made more on the basis of return on investment and not on cost alone. I have often wondered why customers or customer groups are not identified on the company's balance sheet as assets. Are customers not assets? Are they not worthy of investment? Should organizations not require an adequate return on customer investments?

The Be Different service perspective is to serve — not service — customers. It is, in many respects, the same concept as needing to customerize marketing to create an advantage in the marketplace. Consider this as a customerizing approach to servicing the customer.

I am always surprised that an organization's service business is not always considered a critical factor in achieving strategic success. Service has more impact on customer loyalty than any other function of a company. Considering that this element of a business is likely to touch the customer many times each day, it is astonishing how many business leaders do not seem to realize that the service organization holds the success of any strategy in its hands. How many times does your service organization come in contact with your customers on a daily basis? Calculate it yourself to get a perspective on its strategic value to your firm. How many customer *moments of truth* do your service people control each day?

Customerized service = serving the customer.

QUICK HITS

■ Customer service is what the organization wants to supply to the customer; it is governed by policies and rules intended to serve the business.

■ Serving customers, on the other hand, is driven by what the customer wants. The control position is in the customer's hands; the organization is in the responsive position.

■ The service organization is a critical factor in creating customer loyalty and it must receive priority.

Chapter Thirty-Five

Given the service strategic imperative, each organization faces a significant challenge to clearly define how the service organization is going to Be Different in a way that contributes to the company's overall value proposition. The difficulty in extracting strategic value out of the service area is the fact that service is a rather amorphous subject. It means slightly different things to different people.

If you ask ten people what they considered to be good restaurant service, for example, you would get ten slightly different answers. Some would say the quality of the food. Some would say the richness of the wine list. Some would say the ambience of the room. Others would say the personal service they receive. With this array of what customers consider to be good service, it is critical that you begin with a framework that defines exactly what your organization defines service to be, so that a Be Different strategy can be developed.

Some years ago I worked with AchieveGlobal Inc., a service-quality consulting organization, headquartered in Tampa, Florida, with offices in Toronto, Canada, (www.achieveglobal.ca) that helped develop a strategy for service for BC Telecom. The AchieveGlobal Service Quality model was a valuable guide in helping us to move toward a Be Different level of serving customers.

The foundation of their approach was to define service in two components: *Core Service* and the *Service Experience*. AchieveGlobal

204

asserted that this approach would help develop a strategy that would not only be precise and measurable but would also expose opportunities to build customer loyalty.

Core Service is an organization's basic deliverable to the customers it serves. Core service represents the most basic level of what you provide. In many respects it is the foundation upon which your business is built. In the traditional telecommunications business, Core service is defined as dial tone. It doesn't get any more basic than that. Here are some other examples:

- In the finance sector, where most organizations are striving to be successful in providing wealth management services, the core service definition could be defined as financial advice.

- In the computer repair business, it could be a working computer system.

- In the appliance business, it could be appliances that function according to their specifications.

- In the casino business, it could be providing an appropriate mix of gambling games and machines.

- In management consulting, it could be a report that is delivered on time and addresses the requirements defined by the client.

- In the airline business, you might expect core service to be 'the number of take-offs = the number of landings'. After all, if an airline isn't safe, there isn't much point in offering the extras. But how customers perceive an airline's core service may be changing.

  In May 2008, I read that a study about U.S. airlines found that customer satisfaction with the airlines reached its lowest level in seven years due to issues such as lost luggage, flights not leaving on time, higher ticket prices due to rising fuel costs, overbooked flights, charging extra for premium seats and charging extra for more than a single checked bag. Not one person referred to getting to their destination safely. I guess they assume they will.

- In the restaurant business, it could be the quality of the food, the portions, the taste and the presentation.

- In the hotel business, it could be a clean room with common expected amenities such as Internet access, a mini-bar and clean sheets.

Core Service represents the most basic level of what you provide; the foundation upon which your business is built.

The basis of building a Be Different strategy to serve customers is the definition of the core service that your organization provides. This is a tough thing to do. It may appear obvious, but unless you test it with your customers you will not really know for sure. You need to be aware, also, that as your business changes, customers' definitions of what constitutes the core also change. For example, as the telecom business migrates to data applications rather than voice, core service is now defined as 'data tone', or the flawless transmission of data information, rather than traditional dial tone.

The financial industry is transforming itself as well. The traditional core service, defined around savings accounts and interest rates, is now being redefined as financial advice for customers in the wealth management market.

An example from the airline industry underscores this point. Customers expect an airline provider to get them safely to their destination. They also expect their luggage to get there with them, they expect their flight to leave on time and they expect to pay a price that is commensurate with the value they receive. On the latter point, I suspect that the incremental pricing strategy now being employed by airlines to offset rising fuel costs is a major source of customer aggravation. The decision taken by some U.S. airlines to levy a charge to check a single suitcase on domestic flights will do nothing to improve customer satisfaction scores.

The interesting thing about an organization's core service is that if customers are satisfied with it, i.e., if you are meeting their expectations, they reward you by giving you a C on your performance report card, regardless of how much effort you put into it. But don't be fooled into believing that C means that the customer is loyal to you. Your barely adequate grade simply means that they are willing to allow you the opportunity to capture their loyalty in some other way.

People expect a company's core service to work well and work consistently. When I was an operations executive for BC Telecom, I didn't get many calls from customers telling me how delighted they were with the pristine quality of our dial tone. Nor did I get accolades when we spelled their name correctly in the telephone directory or on their monthly bill. If the Blackberry works as the customer expects, you won't get a bouquet of flowers in recognition.

For Core Service, if you meet customer expectations, you get only a C on your report card, regardless of how much effort you put into it.

Similarly, I wouldn't expect a customer of a financial planning institution to be blown away by the fact that they got quality advice from their financial advisor.

What happens, though, when a customer is dissatisfied with your core service?

They complain loudly and long when they try to go online and their Internet service is down. They send letters to the CEO and the media when their name is spelled incorrectly and they have to wait for the next directory publication to see the error remedied. They head for the banks when their credit union financial advisor's sound judgment and advice results in an unexpected drop in the value of their mutual funds.

When core service is not delivered in a satisfactory manner, customers flex their muscles, inflict pain and leave you in a heartbeat. And they never go quietly. They tell whoever will listen to them how bad your organization's service is, and the more people they tell, the happier they are.

Core service, from a customer-loyalty point of view, is a *dissatisfier* in the sense that the customer response is either neutral (you expected what you got) or extremely negative (you didn't). Provide satisfactory core service and the customer will stay with you until a better offer comes along, or until you provide more reasons to stay. Dissatisfy your customers and they leave you, creating pain along the way and a barrier against others coming to you because of their detailed recounting of their negative experience.

If Core Service is not satisfactory, customers flex their muscles, inflict pain and leave you in a heartbeat. And they tell everyone how shoddy your service is.

Organizations need to rethink how they invest to improve service levels. If a company has service issues, it tends to look at increasing core service investments in the belief that increasing customer satisfaction will solve any potential loyalty problem. Investing significant resources into core service is important, but only to get service to satisfactory levels. Even if your customers rate your core service as better than satisfactory, it doesn't assure their loyalty. In fact, any investments made beyond the satisfaction level will not yield a corresponding increase in customer loyalty.

I am not suggesting in any way that organizations should not make investments in core service, or that core service is not an important part of the overall service equation for generating customer loyalty. What I am saying is that satisfactory core service is the ante for playing the service game. Improve it to ensure that it satisfies your customers, but don't invest beyond this level. Investments that will impact customer loyalty should be made to *enhance* the service experience.

QUICK HITS

■ Consider effective customer service to be composed of two elements: core service and the service experience itself, where core service is the basic product or service you provide. Without core service, you simply don't have a business.

■ Your core service is essentially a dissatisfier in the sense that if it meets the expectations of your customers, they are satisfied with your performance and they give you a C rating. You can never do better than a C regardless how pristine your dial tone is. Customers expect your core service to work all the time and they will never give you an A for its performance.

■ If your core service falls short of customer expectations, customers explode. They give you an F, and proudly spread word of their dissatisfaction.

■ The bottom line is that core service is not a source for building customer loyalty, you can't get an A, but you will still lose customers if they are not satisfied with it.

■ Invest in improving core service, but only to the level where it *satisfies* customers. Investments in core service beyond the satisfaction level, with the intent to enhance customer loyalty, will not yield positive returns.

Satisfactory Core Service is the ante for playing the service game. Improve it to the satisfaction level, but don't go beyond.

Chapter Thirty-Six

So what are the considerations in assessing what you have to do to not only improve your core service but also to reinvent it, and where is it necessary to make investments?

Consider reinventing core service rather than simply making incremental improvements to it. Incremental improvements will yield mild results; reinventing core service could yield order of magnitude gains. Customers are worth the effort.

Reinvention not only implies significant change to an existing core service process, but also drives the required changes solely from a customer perspective. It is different from the re-engineering practices that have been traditionally used. Re-engineering, in most changes that I have observed, tends to drive modest incremental process change, and is looked at as a way to achieve cost reduction as opposed to making it easier for a customer to do business with you and at the same time adding value to the transaction.

Reinventing core service begins with an assessment of the core service processes that are an established part of your organization. Core service processes may include handling a customer service inquiry, ordering a service, fulfilling a service request or repairing a product that is deficient in some respect.

Here are some steps you can follow in reinventing your core service processes:

1. What are your core service processes?

   Create an inventory of them in order to gain a more detailed appreciation of the concept as well as to establish a robust information base upon which to begin your reinvention work. This would include customer contact, order placement, order fulfillment, service repair (referred to as 'trouble management' by many) and billing.

Incremental improvements will only yield mild results; reinventing Core Service could yield order of magnitude gains. Customers are worth the effort.

---

2. Which processes are used by your top three customer segments?

   Remember to always consult your Strategic Game Plan in terms of WHO you want to SERVE. You have decided to invest your resources in specific customer segments, so the work you decide to do in serving customers must be consistent with this direction. Always consult your Strategic Game Plan for guidance. Group the core processes for each customer group, and don't be surprised if, for example, Group A has a slightly different list than Group B. After all, we have already concluded that not all customers are equal.

3. Which processes have the highest priority for each customer segment?

   Which have the highest *must matter* factor? Which give the customer the most pain? By all means, get internal views as to which processes particularly annoy customers from your frontline employees who live with the issue on a daily basis. But in the final analysis there is no real substitute for asking the customer. Customer learning here will prove invaluable in determining where your scarce resources should be used to get the greatest payoff.

If your organization has previously institutionalized customer learning, you should already know the weaknesses in your core service operations.

4. What needs to be done to reinvent the highest priority processes?

   Take the number-one priority process for your number-one customer segment and begin the reinvention process. Allocate the time and money necessary to achieve the task, and get on with it. Don't try to boil the ocean. If you are fortunate enough to have sufficient bandwidth to do more than a single process, great. But be aware that taking on too much could jeopardize the entire reinvention work.

Once you have decided on the core service processes you want to reinvent, how do you do it? What does the reinvention process look like?

QUICK HITS

■ Reinvent core service. Don't improve it.

■ Let customers guide the change, not process re-engineering.

■ Inventory your core service processes. Prioritize them and deal first with those that impact your highest value customers.

■ Expect different core service processes for different customer groups.

Chapter Thirty-Seven

The Customer Experience Roadmap

The Customer Experience Roadmap method is a part of the AchieveGlobal Service Quality portfolio and is an excellent way to determine what needs to be changed in order to make a core service process truly customer driven. It is a method of analysis that, for the process chosen, charts each point where the customer comes into contact with your organization.

A simplified example of a customer experience roadmap is illustrated below. The experience begins with the customer contacting the company. In this example, it is via the telephone. The experience continues with the customer interacting with the rep to acquire the information they need in order to make the purchase decision. After the customer places their order, the experience ends with the customer hanging up the telephone and terminating the call. Note that this process is defined completely through the customer's eyes and is redefined each time the customer touches some part of an organization.

The term introduced by Scandinavian Airlines some years back for a customer touch point is 'Moment of Truth'. I like this term, although AchieveGlobal has changed it to 'Defining Moment', because it aptly captures the inherent importance of that moment and describes implicitly the outcomes of either a brilliant interaction with the customer or a disastrous one.

Customer Experience Roadmap

1. The customer calls

2. The customer waits on the line for a rep

3. The customer is connected with a rep

4. The customer obtains service information from the rep

5. The customer orders service from the rep

6. The customer terminates the call

The Customer Experience Roadmap approach creates customer-inspired process reinvention.

The customer experience roadmap method of analysis and re-invention involves the following steps:

- Chart the current state customer-experience process roadmap showing each customer moment, as illustrated in the above example.

- Verify your work by validating the roadmap with your frontline employees and with the customer.

- Look for opportunities to simplify the roadmap. This would typically involve reducing the number of moments of truth to reduce the possibility of things going wrong. The more moments in the roadmap, the higher the probability of error or a process breakdown.

- Look for ways to reduce the complexity of any moment of truth. For example, if the moment involves the customer placing an order for service, make it easy to do. Engage the customer briefly in the moment and make it painless. Use technology for those who like to do it themselves, but don't force it on everyone. Simple is good; simpler is better.

- At the other end of the spectrum, look for opportunities to enhance a moment, to provide more value to the customer. For example, be open to problem solving with your customers if they want to enquire about their bill. Provide your customers with information regarding new product offerings when they are requesting service, or allow them to place an order for a new service when they are reporting a service problem. But be careful when looking for enhancing opportunities. The moment needs to be simple; it needs to contain the critical *must-have* elements and it cannot under any circumstances contain company *push* elements that don't line up with customer acceptance. This will produce a *de-dazzling* event.

QUICK HITS

- The customer experience roadmap approach drives process reinvention from the customer's point of view.

- Chart the roadmap that customers experience; make sure it meets customer expectations by designing each moment of truth with the customer in mind.

Chapter Thirty-Eight

Service Level Differentiation

The ultimate effect of creating core service processes that reflect the unique requirements of different customer segments is service level differentiation: creating different core service processes and, hence, levels of service for the various customer groups that your organization has decided to serve. If done properly, higher value customers will experience a greater, more customized and personal level of service than customer groups that provide lower value to the organization.

Service Level Differentiation = different core service for different customer groups.

Most organizations provide one level of service and that's it. Take it or leave it. This is unfortunate because differentiating core service processes based on customer value is very practical and has a dramatic impact on how your customers see you and how committed you are to serving them well. There are a number of generic areas to differentiate core service levels:

- How customers contact your organization. As opposed to a common 1-800 number for every customer to access, dedicate a special one for your high-value customers.

- How the sales process is executed. Perhaps mass market customers get a telemarketing call; special customers get a sales visit.

- How a service breakdown is handled. Assign a unique call-in number to high-end clients; everyone else shares a common number.

- How relationships are managed. For example, the top ten get a call from the CEO every six months to see how things are going; everyone else gets a relationship call from a call center rep every twelve months. Remember your top customers' special life-events such as birthdays, anniversaries, etc., and send a personalized handwritten note to recognize those special days.

- How after-sales service is handled. Top customers get a follow-up call immediately after purchasing a product or service; others get a call within three days.

- How you communicate with special customer groups. If you have a significant concentration of immigrant customers in a particular area, for example, advise them to call a specific number for service, and have a rep available who speaks their native language. At BC Telecom, we always tried to match the profile of our service reps to the demographics of the customer base being served.

Don't conclude that differentiating core service levels is about providing great service to the upper tier of customers and substandard service to everyone else. The objective is to serve your customers in the best possible manner and then reserve elite service for those who deserve it due to the profits they provide your organization. Higher value customers require higher levels of service investment; it just makes economic sense.

For example, BC Telecom served only their highest value business clients in the following ways:

- We provided a dedicated telephone number for each customer to call to report a service problem with either their equipment or network.

- Clients could request a service installation date convenient to their schedules. This proved to be a significant challenge, given the complexities of coordinating schedules, but it was well worth the effort. As an aside, most utility-type organizations still have difficulty doing this; in fact the norm is that they tell you when you can have the service.

- Dedicated teams of sales and service professionals were assigned specific clients, and it was the professionals' responsibility to 'take care of them no matter what.' Each client knew the people on their personal sales and service team by name and could contact them for any reason.

Higher value customers require higher levels of service investment. It makes good economic sense.

Reinventing core processes to deliver these types of capabilities was non-trivial but the results were impressive. In the end, we created an organization, Business Communications Services, which was dedicated to serving the highest value businesses in B.C. Service results were strong, and we made significant inroads to growing our customer share with many of the clients who were served in this fashion. Our prices were not the lowest in the market, but clients rewarded our higher service investments by giving us more of their business. A definite win-win.

QUICK HITS

■ In the Marketing Section, we discussed the importance of segmenting your customer base to identify distinct customer groups with varying characteristics and value to the organization. Core service processes need to be designed with this segmentation in mind.

■ High value customer groups should have different core service processes than other customer groups; it's an investment that makes good sense.

■ Service level differentiation is an effective way to build customer loyalty and grow your share of wallet.

■ Your competitors might offer one level of service to everyone; Be Different and break from the pack.

Chapter Thirty-Nine

The Service Experience: Do You Want Loyal Customers?

As explained in Chapter Thirty-Five, core service is what customers get from you. The *Service Experience*, on the other hand, describes how they feel when they get it. This component of the service equation is the driver of customer loyalty.

Everyone can relate to their own experience when recalling an example of exemplary customer service. When you are in a restaurant enjoying your meal (is food the core service to the fine dining business?) and the server is not only knowledgeable in terms of the menu items, but friendly, thoughtful, responsive and anticipates your every need, how do you feel? I use terms like blown away, smitten, delighted and dazzled. Sure the food was good, but the level of service was so personal that you can't stop talking about it and you look forward to enjoying this experience again and again and again.

Core Service is what customers get from you, the Service Experience describes how they feel when they get it.

I observe that people judge service experiences against their best service anywhere, for anything and provided by anyone. So, if you're in the retail business and a customer who has had the 'greatest service experience ever' in a restaurant comes into your store, your challenge is not only to out-serve your retail competition, it's to be the best across all service contenders in the market.

What causes this dazzled reaction from a customer? Basically, you moved beyond what they expected from you to a level beyond their expectations. You dazzled them because you gave them what they didn't expect. It's kind of counterintuitive in that the *WOW* factor comes from NOT giving a customer only what they want; but from surprising them.

So what do you get in return? Unlike core service ratings, a dazzled customer will most certainly give you an A for your efforts and will keep coming back.

And do they tell others how great you are? Absolutely. Do you realize how many times I have told the story of Rita and Rodeo Jewellers in Vancouver, and of the Spaghetti Factory in Whistler (Section One, Chapter Seven)? Viral marketing created by the service organization, who would have thought it?

A dazzled customer gives you an A for your efforts and remains loyal. Each time they are delighted, smitten, wowed or blown away, their breath is taken away and they laud you with accolades befitting someone of royal stature.

Looking to invest in improving service? Make sure your core service infrastructure can consistently satisfy your customers and then pour on the coals to enable your service team to dazzle them. This is the area that produces healthy returns on investment because it creates a loyal customer base and an annuity revenue stream for a long time.

Remember, the service experience is not only influenced by the human factor in an organization, but also by technology. Technology has a big impact on how customers feel when they try to do business with your organization. So take a look at the technology that interfaces with your customers to ensure that the experience they feel is dazzling. (Dazzling technology: an oxymoron?)

I think one of the most common technology interfaces that most companies use these days is Integrated Voice Response (IVR)technology. I would also venture to guess that this technology represents one of the main frustrations customers encounter when trying to contact any business or organization by phone. Unfortunately, this is a common complaint from people who are directed away from a *high touch* human interface to a *high tech* one. It's not feasible for every customer to be served by an actual person for every request made — and decision tree algorithms are a reality for businesses today — but you must create the high tech service experience with the principles that guide building customer loyalty in mind.

QUICK HITS

- Whereas core service is what customers get from your organization, the *Service Experience* is how they feel when they get it.

- The service experience, unlike core service, is the driver of customer loyalty. If customers are dazzled by you, they will give you an A, stay with you and tell others how great you are.

- Investments intended to improve the customer experience make sense; they will produce handsome returns.

Chapter Forty

If dazzling customers is strategically important to every organization, how is it accomplished?

In Chapter Thirty-Eight, we discussed the importance of providing special levels of core service for your higher value customer segments. The *Vary the Treatment* idea advocated by the AchieveGlobal folks takes this approach to an individual level and asks the question, 'What can I do to provide each individual customer with a dazzling service experience?'

The Vary the Treatment principle is based on the fact that providing the same level of service to everyone will satisfy some customers, but will dissatisfy others. Why? Because each person is different; what service level satisfies one customer may not satisfy another. If, on the other hand, you provide variable levels of service, you get a constant level of customer satisfaction with each of your customers and a greater chance of building their loyalty.

Dazzling a customer requires a flexible service approach. Customer-contact employees or high-tech touch points must be able to flex to what each customer expects during a moment of truth. This becomes exceedingly difficult, sometimes impossible, in the high tech world of customer interaction, where flexible treatment and outcomes must be studied beforehand and programmed into the interaction device.

Artificial intelligence in a real-time service situation where customer loyalty is on the line is no substitute for human intellect and problem solving.

In sum, this is the Vary the Treatment formula:

- *Same service experience* = variable levels of customer satisfaction = inconsistent loyalty building

- *Variable service experience* = constant levels of satisfaction = consistent loyalty building

Here are four practical steps you can take to Vary the Treatment:

Vary how you treat customers to dazzle them. Treating them all the same way is a de-dazzling experience for many, and doesn't promote widespread loyalty.

Rule #1 — Hire human being lovers

Ever been treated in a store by an individual that you suspected has an extreme dislike for human beings? You know the type: disgruntled, cranky and totally disinterested in you and in what you want. Unfortunately, they are in every organization these days; just one minute with one of these people destroys all previous loyalty building efforts. Since people generally control the service experience (as noted above, technology has its limitations in dazzling people), it follows that organizations should be hiring and developing individuals with this aptitude and orientation.

Take a look at your recruitment processes for hiring customer-contact employees. How rigorous are they in terms of seeking the best of the best in creating memorable experiences for customers? Ironically, in most organizations, these frontline positions are ranked relatively low in value; the requisites for the job are not terribly demanding and the interview guides for such positions don't really probe the human-to-human aspect of the job.

Even when I held executive positions in operations I would make a point of getting involved in the hiring process. This sent out a strong message to my entire organization that these were important positions and that if I could allocate my time to it so could they. I have asked the following questions when interviewing for a frontline position.

Do you like human beings? Ask potential frontliners this question straight up. They will discover it is not a trick question, but clearly one that declares the human qualities you want.

- Do you like human beings? Ask this question directly. They will soon discover that it is not a trick question but rather sets the tone for the entire interview, and clearly declares the human qualities you are interested in.

- What are some examples where you have gone the extra mile for someone else? How often have you done it? Why did you do it? How did it feel? How did the other person feel?

- How good are you at dazzling others? What are the best examples of where you have done it?

- Dazzle me by saying something. Seriously.

- How do you deal with conflict? Remember, even though a customer may be screaming their head off at a frontliner, a dazzling experience is still the objective, and it can still be done.

- What other service positions have you held in the past, and who were your employers? If, for example, the person worked for a good service-oriented business then you might expect that they would have the ability to do the job. If, on the other hand, the person worked for an organization with a bad service reputation, you might conclude the opposite.

- What service training have you had that deals with delighting customers? We created a Service Quality training program during my tenure at BC Telecom. It provided an overview of the principles of serving customers to build loyalty — the contents of this book — and was mandatory for frontline service people and for management. Break-out sessions were an essential part of the program design and allowed individuals to practice the behaviors they were taught, with feedback and critique from others in the workshop.

• In previous service positions, what was your compensation plan and how was your performance measured? Companies that take service seriously pay their people for service performance; a substantial portion of their bonus pay is based on service results. Furthermore, the service measurement system used is based on customer perception rather than on internal statistics. Customer perception is reality, regardless of what your employees might say.

Can you train someone to be great at serving customers? For example, you hire someone into a customer service rep position who has demonstrated arithmetic skills, has experience in a call-center environment selling products and services, and displays good team skills. But the person is deficient in interpersonal relationship skills. Can you train this person to dazzle customers, which entails inherent people-empathizing and caring abilities?

I have trouble believing that training can effectively fill the gap. You either like people or you don't. You can't teach people to *love humans*. You either have a high pain threshold or you don't. You can't teach people to *love pain.* You either care about people's issues or you don't. You can't teach people to care about others.

You can't train people to like humans. They are born with the strength; go find them and hire them.

I believe that if you want employees who can dazzle customers you need to hire people with the innate ability to do it. Train them on other aspects of the job, like job content, but hire them for their people-loving bias. Get Human Resources to revamp the frontline employee acquisition methodology, complete with prerequisites, skills, experience and interviewing guide. Get it on their performance plan. Make it matter.

Rule #2 — Bend the rules; empower the frontliners to say yes

Here is a simple question: How easy is it for a frontline employee to dazzle a customer when they are saying no to what the customer wants? In many situations, frontline employees are placed in the position of having to police the rules and policies of the organization. In some organizations, frontline employees cannot deviate from them; in some, they are punished if they do. Trying to enforce rules that are unacceptable to a customer is a recipe for creating a de-dazzling event; the customer is upset with you and, of course, tells many others how insensitive you are.

Given the variability of customer needs and expectations, the desired service state is to allow frontline people to bend the rules in favor of the customer and allow them to *say yes*, as opposed to being put in a rule enforcement mode all the time and having to say no.

Frontline people must be allowed to bend the rules in favor of the customer. They need to say yes, as opposed to being put in a rule-enforcement mode all the time and saying no.

Empowering frontline people to say yes is not always met with enthusiasm. There is often significant skepticism and distrust of the process. Executives sometimes view this as a loss of control; frontline (read junior) employees 'will sell the farm if we allow them to do this' is often cited as a reason for not letting go.

In my experience, these concerns are grossly overstated and generally unfounded. What you find is that frontline employees really do care about the company and about doing the things that ensure that it remains financially healthy. You will find that they will not cave in to every customer; rather, in those exceptional cases where rules should be bent in order for a customer to get what they want, and for the company to continue to get their revenue, employees will do it in a way that minimizes the deviation from the rule and the risk exposure to the company. They will do it in a way that keeps the loyalty train moving.

At one point in my career with BC Telecom, I was responsible for the Credit and Collections function, an area fraught with the challenges one would expect to see in an area associated with this aspect of finance. It is no surprise that the Credit and Collections representative had the challenging task of trying to apply company policy while at the same time maintaining a high level of customer satisfaction. All representatives were rated on service provided in their performance plan. In an effort to do the right thing, we basically changed the position-responsibility description from managing credit to managing risk. We introduced a new set of behaviors and expectations that were more in keeping with treating the customer in a more flexible manner while containing financial risk.

Organizations must establish boundaries within which empowerment can happen, and let frontliners have a go at it.

I suggest that organizations establish some boundaries within which empowerment can happen, and let frontliners have a go at it. Monitor their performance. Empowering frontline employees will achieve three goals:

- It will delight customers and lead to enhanced customer loyalty.

- It will significantly enhance employee morale and confidence, knowing that the organization's leadership trusts that they have the best interests of the organization at heart.

- It will not result in negative financials for the company; frontliners do not sell the organization down the river.

Empowering frontliners to bend the existing rules in favor of the customer is one part of the solution. The ultimate solution is to only develop your portfolio of rules, policies and processes around customer expectations, and minimize the amount of bending-the-rule behavior.

Rule #3 — Kill dumb rules

Principle #1 – New service guidelines should be constructed to empower the frontliners to say yes to customers as opposed to saying no.

Principle #2 – Eliminate 50% of your dumb rules over the next ninety days; customer loyalty is vulnerable.

A dumb rule: a rule, process or policy that makes zero sense to a customer. It has been created in the company's best interest, not to serve the customer.

What is a dumb rule? It is a rule, process or policy that simply does not make any sense to the customer. It exists within a customer service system that has been created to apply to the customer rather than to enable or serve the customer. It may be a policy to do with purchasing a product or service, administering credit or using a service. Regardless, it is a situation where the boundaries imposed on the customer by the company simply do not resonate with the people paying the bill. Does your organization have any such rules? If you say no, then you haven't looked close enough, and you certainly haven't asked your frontline employees or your customers.

Here are some examples of dumb rules:

- In a restaurant you are seated where there is a server, as opposed to where you would like to sit. To make matters worse, when you ask the hostess if you could possibly sit 'over there', you get a look that could stop a train. As customers, our role is not to make life easier for the servers, *but* as someone who keeps them in business.

- Imagine that you and your wife enter a casual dining spot late at night after gambling in a high-end hotel and casino resort, in Las Vegas. You are hungry for one of their delicious Reuben sandwiches. The place is virtually empty and you ask to be seated in a booth. You are advised by the hostess that it is not possible to satisfy your request because booths are reserved for parties of three or more. *But* there are no other customers in the place; how can seating a couple in a booth cause a problem? Beats me. Just another dumb rule, and they forgot to empower the hostess to break the rule if it made sense for the customer.

- You are in a conversation with a rep in a call center getting information on a product that you are interested in. You are late for a meeting and you have to get off the call so you ask if they can e-mail the product information to you. They advise you that they are unable to comply with your request; it is against policy to communicate in written form to a customer. Anyway, they don't have access to e-mail service even if they were allowed to do it. You are then required to call back (of course, you won't get the same rep), repeat your story and copy down the information you need. Too bad. All they really needed to do was to direct you to their website, if it contains the detailed information.

Does your organization have any dumb rules? If you say no, then you haven't looked close enough, and you haven't asked your frontline employees or your customers.

- Refusing to extend a credit-card limit temporarily to an individual with sufficient financial resources who is making a retail purchase. This one drives me crazy. For some reason, you have gone beyond your credit card limit and you need some flexibility. You want the vendor to understand your plight and give you a break, because you can pay for the purchase. But no. The policy says that you have exceeded your limit, so that's that. I think that if you use your card a lot, the credit card company should know you. Shouldn't they? It is not too difficult to track your purchases (customer learning) and have intimate knowledge of your income (customer secrets) and to use this information to make the right decision. That is, in favor of the customer. Imagine the power in the statement 'I'm sorry, Mr. Osing, but you have exceeded your credit card limit with this purchase. But, no worries, we will extend your limit to take care of this. How much more do you need?' I would be blown away to be treated this way.

There has to be a more customer-friendly way for organizations to manage credit risk. Rather than protecting their backside, they could use this as an opportunity to dazzle customers and build loyalty.

- A large wireless communications company in Canada insists that a new mobility customer use their service for at least six months in Canada before using their cellular phone in Europe. The issue here is that certain providers offer phones that work on the wireless technology in Europe, while others do not. A TELUS customer, I was looking to this company's service temporarily while I was on vacation. I understand why the policy is there: the company does not want to take on a credit risk and have to face a significant bad debt problem if I happen to run up a huge bill in Europe and not pay it. I called a colleague, who is the president of the organization, and he fixed it for me. But I had a bad taste in my mouth from my original encounter with their service rep.

There has to be a more customer-friendly way for organizations to manage credit risk. Rather than protecting their backside, they could have used this as an opportunity to win a customer. Rather than restrict service, a better approach would have been to tell me why they have the rule, and then ask me some questions that would help the rep assess my risk and try to acquire me as a customer.

- A rule with the same intent as the previous example was to limit the amount of service to a new customer until the customer has shown that they can pay their bill. I was involved in this particular situation as the executive responsible for the credit organization in BC Telecom. I received a call from an angry customer who had just moved to B.C. He had been told that, since he had not been a resident of B.C. for at least twelve months, he was limited to $100 in long distance calls per month. After six months (read this as 'once we trust that you will pay your bill') he would be allowed to use our LD service as much as he wanted. As things turned out, he was an executive of a financial institution and represented minimal credit risk to us. But this particular event was instrumental in driving us to revise how we viewed the job of the credit rep within our organization. Rather than enforcing the credit rules of the company, we changed the role to managing credit risk, with credit guidelines replacing rigid rules. The rep was empowered to make the right decision for the customer, which would create customer loyalty. The reps took their new responsibility seriously; credit problems went down and customer satisfaction skyrocketed.

Know a dumb rule? Share it with me at www. bedifferentorbedead.com

---

- A financial institution had a unique rule when it came to procuring U.S. funds. I knew I was in trouble when the teller asked me if I had called ahead to 'order' the U.S. funds that I wanted. I had not, and she advised me that, due to past robberies that seemed to focus on U.S. rather than Canadian funds, they didn't keep significant U.S. funds at the branch. She also informed me that she couldn't fill my entire order because she needed to keep some funds for other customers. The bottom line was that I only got a portion of the amount I wanted and was forced to go to another branch, which did fill my order. That branch had U.S. funds in abundance; they had solved their security challenge without causing pain to their customers. First, an understanding of differentiating service levels based on customer value might have suggested that I should have been given the entire amount I needed, as opposed to being given only a portion. Second, I the customer was expected to solve their security risk. Bottom line: this dumb rule exposes a number of Be Different vulnerabilities.

Dumb rules abound in all organizations. Everyone has an abundance of dumb rules. But don't take my word for it. Go ask your own frontline people for examples of dumb rules. You will be surprised at what they tell you.

Set up a Dumb Rules Committee to seek out, destroy or otherwise modify things that don't make any sense to customers.

The Be Different service proposition is that in situations where your processes, rules or policies are dysfunctional from a customer perspective, eliminate them, or at the very least re-vector them to make them customer friendly. Avoid treating your most valued customers as second class citizens. Think of this as 'cleansing the internal environment' of things that don't make customer sense.

I had a lot of fun addressing this challenge during my career in operations. I mobilized dumb rules committees in the various departments of the company: marketing, sales, finance, customer service and so on. The chairperson had a mandate to seek out, destroy or otherwise modify things that were senseless to customers.

Committees were empowered to bring rules issues to management. Management was obligated to get back to a committee with a response in terms of an action to be taken; the action had to be in favor of the customer. We had contests among the dumb rules committees to see which could discover the dumbest rule, and which could then take the action that turned it into a positive for the customer.

The Operator Services team at TELUS, in the BC Telecom days, was the continuous winner of these contests; the team was traditionally one of the most rule-bound groups in the company and had an abundance of rules to put forth. They were one of the most customer-focused groups I have ever had the pleasure of being associated with. They were passionate about making it easier for the customer to do business with us, and would go the extra mile to show it.

Dumb Rules: if you can't eliminate them, make them customer friendly.

The Dumb Rules Committee approach is effective in correcting current rule and policy dysfunction within the organization. But organizations need a model to guide the development of customer-inspired rules, policies and procedures on an ongoing basis.

The long term solution is to construct processes, rules and policies in the image of the customer, as opposed to the image of the company (the inside view). The logic is compelling: if you have rules and policies that enable the customer to transact business with you on their terms you avoid de-dazzling events and retain a loyal customer base. Don't forget they tell others about how great you are. It sounds simple enough, which makes you wonder why so many organizations don't pay any attention to it.

Some will say that building rules and policies from a customer point of view will not work in every case; that there are legal and perhaps regulatory issues that require specific rules to be imposed on customers. This is true, and I am not advocating anything that would jeopardize your organization. If you have specific rules and policies that are founded in legal requirements, try to articulate them in a customer-sensitive way, and ensure that your frontline organization is trained to explain them to customers in an empathetic way — as opposed to coming across as 'policy police'. If the customer understands the rule and why you must follow it, a good relationship can still be maintained.

Assign a dumb rules executive champion; communicate progress internally and make it matter to people.

To make this matter to your organization, assign a senior leader (I was the dumb rules champion in our company) the task of making the organization more sensitive to customers and to implementing programs such as dumb rules committees. Talk about it constantly in your internal media; reinforce the idea that 'cleansing for the customer' is an essential part of your strategy. Honor those employees who exhibit a passion for managing dumb rules sensitively and who, thereby, got the message out to others in the company.

Rule #4 — Recover: Fix it and do the unexpected

Probably the most powerful idea I learned from AchieveGlobal is the notion of Service Recovery, which defines the fourth Vary the Treatment principle in creating a dazzling service experience for your customers. Recovery deals with how your organization manages a service breakdown, a broken customer promise or a mistake that resulted in a customer being extremely angry and dissatisfied with your organization. Ever have any of these happen to you? Ever make mistakes? Oh yes. It's your response that counts. How you respond to the breakdown or broken promise can have a substantial effect, dazzling the customer and building their loyalty.

The concept of service recovery addresses the power of responding to mistakes in the right manner, and completes the formula that defines how customer loyalty is built.

Don't punish mistakes; treat them as loyalty-building opportunities.

Here is the formula:

Customer Loyalty = Mind Blowing Experiences when things go right + Unbelievable Recovery when things go wrong

Let me explain. The first part of the equation represents the service experience factor discussed earlier and assumes that your core service is satisfactory. There is another driver of loyalty, however, and it is rather perverse: it deals with the power of dealing with an unintended service breakdown or blunder in the organization. When I ask people to recall their most unfortunate service experience, they are likely to tell a recovery story, rather than an experience when everything went right. What sticks in the customer's mind seems to be how an organization responds when it makes a mistake, rather than how it invariably delivers error-free service.

Service Recovery is the art of fixing a mistake or problem that your organization has made, and going on to do the unexpected for the customer.

Service Recovery = Fix It + Do The Unexpected

Most organizations get the first part of this. While they understand the need to fix a mistake, they often don't understand that they get no real strategic value, i.e., loyalty building, from doing that. Customers expect the issue will be resolved to their satisfaction and simply say, 'Good.' But it should never have happened in the first place. It sounds like our discussion around core service, doesn't it? That is, if you don't fix it, there is a good chance the customer will simply leave you for some other company, and tell everyone how terrible your service is.

Going beyond merely fixing it is mandatory if you want to build loyalty. If you recover well after a service breakdown you actually have a more loyal customer than if the breakdown hadn't happened at all. Some of you astute strategists out there will suddenly land on the insight that if you *cause* strategic errors to occur in your organization you can jump on them, recover well and build loyalty. I wouldn't suggest this approach; humans and technology are likely to make mistakes without any intervention on your part.

If you recover well after a service breakdown, you have a more loyal customer than if the breakdown hadn't happened at all.

The good news is that if you understand how to recover you can turn a potentially de-dazzling event into a remarkable one that helps build your business.

Recovery is so important that you need a plan to create the capability throughout your organization. Here are the four steps to developing a Service Recovery Plan:

1. **Acknowledgement.** Admit to the customer that the mistake has been made and accept responsibility for it. Customers don't want to hear that it wasn't your fault; they don't want to hear that it was the responsibility of another department. They want to hear that you are taking responsibility to make right what has gone wrong.

2. **Atonement.** This is all about atoning for your sins and usually involves a tangible way of saying you're sorry. It doesn't have to be complicated, but it must be heartfelt. For example, when I was leading a large operating division, we made gift certificates available to credit reps to use if we ran into trouble managing a customer's credit plan. To keep this under a certain amount of control, we established an 'Atonement Plan', which defined what type of recognition should be provided to a customer under various circumstances.

The Atonement Plan should be based on the principle that the more serious the error is to the customer — particularly when the customer generates high revenue for your business — the more elaborate, and perhaps expensive, the atonement. For example, if your number-one customer had a problem with your product or service that caused them significant discomfort for two days, you should consider doing something special to atone. You would provide lesser recognition to a smaller customer suffering a less serious problem.

Recovery: Do it more than right the second time, and do it fast.

3. **Resolution.** This is the fix-it stage. The problem must be resolved to the customer's satisfaction. Take every opportunity to allow the customer to see what is being done to make amends. Communicate constantly with them during the fix-it phase. They will be impressed, both because you care enough to keep them informed and because you have mobilized the resources of your organization on their behalf.

4. **Surprise.** This step in the process deals up the unexpected. If the process has gone along as it should, the customer is now mildly favorable toward you. The problem has been fixed, which is the core service component of service recovery, you have apologized, taken full responsibility for the breakdown and provided a token gesture of your regret. The customer is definitely leaning your way. Now is the time to blow 'em away, to surprise them by doing something or by providing them with something they simply would not expect. This is not to be confused with *the ultimate atonement* factor. This is not an expression of regret as atonement is; rather, this is an act that is related to your recognition of the fact that the customer is valued for their long term contribution to your business. It is an investment that will support the ongoing revenue stream you expect to get from that customer.

This is the most difficult step in the recovery process, but it is the most critical. If it is done well, loyalty is enhanced. It requires a very special knowledge of the customer in order to surprise them. The source of knowledge to execute this *surprise factor* is directly related to the customer secrets your organization has discovered. The more you know about the customer, the better your capability to surprise them. The customer expects you to resolve the problem you have created; they will *not* expect you to go beyond that, to do something special, something in which you had to invest time and energy. I guarantee that if you do this well you will get this customer response, 'Wow I can't believe they did this for me.' This is the dazzle factor.

Successful recovery is all about surprise. If you can't surprise 'em you can't recover well.

Time is of the essence to get the full loyalty-building impact of recovery. The figure below illustrates the relationship between loyalty building and time to recover. It shows that during the first twenty-four hours after a service problem, loyalty grows very quickly. The customer's commitment to your organization is stronger than prior to the service problem. They are dazzled with the experience they are having while you fix the problem. After twenty-four hours, the customer's 'wow, this is impressive' feeling quickly wanes and their strong feelings of commitment to you decline. Loyalty is destroyed. The bottom line is that you have less than twenty-four hours to execute the recovery process to get the full loyalty effects. After twenty-four hours you've lost it.

Does your organization have a recovery strategy? Most organizations don't, which is surprising, given its importance. I suggest that you review the strategic plan for your business and find a way to start the recovery plan process. It doesn't have to be perfect; the critical thing is that you begin the process and learn what works and what doesn't work, and make adjustments as you go. Later, we will discuss the importance of creating a Service Strategy for your organization and include recovery explicitly, as a critical component of it.

RECOVERY

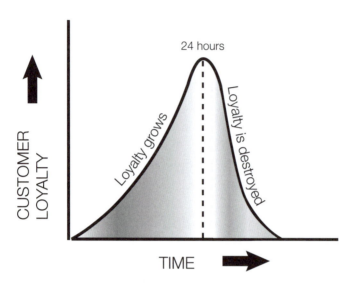

You have less than twenty-four hours to execute the recovery process and get its full loyalty effects. After twenty-four hours you've lost it.

A very important part of any recovery strategy is communicating its importance to the entire organization. Do it from the top. If a key executive is assigned to be the Recovery Champion, everyone will notice and will correctly conclude that recovery is a vital component of your overall strategy. Integrate it into all your employee communication vehicles, saturate the internal media with the message. Recognize employees who have contributed to a successful recovery, honor them in a very special way — others will want to 'get a piece of the action', and your Recovery performance will improve dramatically.

Memorable recovery experiences?

The Spaghetti Factory in Whistler, Canada (refer back to Chapter Seven: Look in Every Nook and Cranny for Your Edge). You make a mistake and you pay for it graciously and generously.

Here's a recent story involving my wife and me as we attempted to fly home from Ganges, Saltspring Island, during our 2008 vacation. We booked a flight with Harbour Air (www.harbourair.com), which operates a seaplane business serving many locations on the west coast of B.C. We were scheduled to leave Ganges at 9:30 a.m., destined for the Vancouver Airport. I called Harbour Air at 9:00 a.m. to confirm the flight and was told that it was delayed to 10:15 a.m. 'Are you absolutely sure that the flight is now going at 10:15?' I asked.

'Yes, sir; definitely,' I was told.

Assign a key executive to be the recovery champion; everyone will notice and will correctly conclude that recovery is a vital component of your overall strategy.

At 10:15, I was out on the dock anxiously looking for our plane. It was, of course, nowhere in sight. I decided to check the voicemails on my TELUS mobile. There was a message from Saltspring Air informing me that Harbour Air had contacted them and asked them to handle our flight to the Vancouver Airport. Saltspring Air had expected us for their 9:30 a.m. flight. But since we were a 'no show', they had left without us. Nice. While it was gratifying to hear that Harbour Air was creative enough to ask Saltspring Air to handle the Ganges to Vancouver flight, presumably because they had an insufficient load, they should have closed the creative loop by telling the customer they had done it. My call to Harbour Air resulted in this recovery:

- They acknowledged and sincerely apologized for their mistake.

- They re-booked us on the 10:45 a.m. Saltspring Air flight to Downtown Vancouver.

- They gave us a 50% discount on our flight rate. The value reduction was at least 50%, so the marketing side of me said this made sense.

- They arranged for a taxi to take us home to White Rock from Downtown Vancouver, and they paid for it — $93.

- When I reached their ticket counter in Vancouver to get the taxi voucher, everyone knew us and about the service breakdown. Again more acknowledgement of our pain, and an admission of their responsibility for causing it and their sincere apologies for it.

Harbour Air on the west coast of B.C. clearly understands the power of recovery.

Not a bad recovery. The only thing that could have been handled better was prior approval of the recovery actions that they took. The Harbour Air rep that I talked to had to go off-line and discuss the matter with a manager, who then made the decision on what the organization was prepared to do. It would have been a much more powerful and dazzling experience for me had the rep been empowered to determine the appropriate recovery plan herself, with me on the phone. Having said that, I applaud Harbour Air for what they did, and I told them so.

Postscript to this story. What did Saltspring Air get out of the Harbour Air mishap? Well, they had a competitor's customers on their aircraft and they chose to represent themselves as the little guy who always runs their flights on time, not denigrating Harbour Air in any way while saying it, and who are very sensitive to making it easy for people who flew with them. The pilot decided to drop us off at the Harbour Air float, which was located some ten to fifteen walking minutes away from its own terminal. He could have taken us to their terminal and we would have had to walk back to Harbour Air. But the pilot chose not to. Looked like an attempted 'loyalty assault' by the Saltspring Air pilot. Impressive. And it may just have worked, as my wife and I have a very warm feeling about a seaplane organization we didn't even know existed before the Harbour Air incident.

QUICK HITS

- How do you dazzle your customers? Vary the way you treat them. They are all individuals with different expectations, so be prepared to treat each of them differently.

- Here is the four-step Vary the Treatment process:

  1. Hire people who honestly like to deal with humans. You can't train them to like people, you have to find them and hire them.

  2. Allow frontliners to bend your rules; empower them to say yes to customers rather than to simply enforce company policy. Nothing blows a customer away more than seeing your employee break their own rule in order to do what the customer wants.

  3. Get rid of policies, rules and procedures that don't make sense to customers, that, in fact, annoy them. If a dumb rule can't be eliminated, at least make it customer friendly and explain why it exists.

  4. Implement a Service Recovery strategy: a process of fixing a service breakdown or mistake and then doing the unexpected. Nothing dazzles a customer like mind-blowing recovery. But you only have a limited time to do it; if you can't recover in less than twenty-four hours, a dazzling opportunity turns into a service disaster.

Chapter Forty-One

To this point, we have discussed the two components of serving customers. One, Core Service and two, the Service Experience and what organizations need to do to morph service into the Be Different realm. The bottom line is that serving customers successfully requires that you create the core service capabilities to meet their transaction needs and expectations, and that you provide a dazzling service experience. A dazzling experience delivered with a core service process that is unacceptable to the customer destroys loyalty, and an acceptable core service with a disastrous service experience does the same thing.

Loyalty building = satisfactory Core Service + dazzling Service Experience.

The AchieveGlobal dictum is that you need to do both:

- Satisfy (meet expectations of) the customer with your core service, and

- Dazzle (exceed expectations of) the customer with their service experience with you.

GOAL IS TO DAZZLE

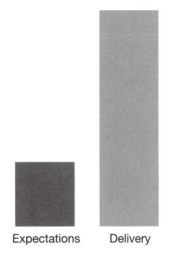

GOAL IS TO SATISFY

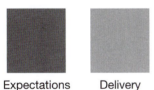

Expectations   Delivery   Expectations   Delivery

CORE SERVICE   **SERVICE EXPERIENCE**

QUICK HITS

■ A dazzling service experience with unsatisfactory core service destroys customer loyalty.

■ Satisfactory core service and an acceptable service experience does nothing to build loyalty.

■ Dazzle = blow 'em away on the experience *and* satisfy 'em on the core service.

Chapter Forty-Two

Create Your Service Strategy

Another plank in the AchieveGlobal Service Quality platform, and the challenge you now face, is to choose the specific attributes of service that you want your organization to focus on and to invest in. The task is to answer the question, 'In the world of serving customers, what do I want to be famous for?' The answer to this question defines your *Service Strategy*.

The development of a service strategy for your organization is extremely important; it provides a service destination for your entire team and avoids the problem of everyone providing customers what they, personally, think is good service. In Section Two earlier, we discussed the importance of FOCUS. FOCUS. FOCUS. Well, it certainly applies here, because there is a significant potential for people to do their own service *thing*.

Your service strategy must reflect both elements of core service and the service experience discussed in the last chapter:

- Core service elements to satisfy

- Service experience elements to dazzle.

What will be your focus in providing core service? Which aspects will you concentrate on, given the various customer segments that you have chosen to serve? In the service experience component, which aspects will you develop and target, given the importance of creating customer loyalty?

Your Service Strategy provides a service destination for your entire team and avoids everyone providing customers what they, personally, think good service is.

This was the service strategy we developed when I was VP of the Business Communications Division (BCD) at BC Telecom.

> 'We are easy to do business with. We care.
>
> We provide and support innovative quality solutions.
>
> We make promises and always keep them.
>
> If we fall short of our strategy, RECOVERY will be our #1 priority.'

This strategy demonstrates the commitment to providing satisfactory core service: 'We provide and support innovative quality solutions.' This statement says a lot. The quality reference relates to the traditional Total Quality Management (TQM) principle of 'conforming to requirements' — for example, having your product perform exactly to specifications. What other core service references are contained in this statement?

- First, it uses the term *solutions* rather than products or services, which emphasizes creating value for customers based on their overall requirements or challenges, rather than on flogging products.

- Second, it gives criteria for the solutions: they must be *innovative*, and demonstrate a deep understanding of your customers and what they need.

- Third, the commitment to *support* quality solutions ensures that customers get the after-sales attention they expect.

- Fourth, the 'easy to do business with' reference gives direction to the business systems and processes in the organization; these must be developed to enable the customer to conduct business in an enjoyable manner, rather than be frustrated.

- Fifth, reference to 'making promises and always keeping them' informs the success criteria of delivering to customer expectations that were promised. This includes such things as time commitments made, product quality and the availability of support services.

The service experience strategy states that *We Care*, introducing the high touch factor for customer-contact employees. It also establishes the same guide for the technology that may be used to manage customers who call in to the organization. The 'easy to do business with' phrase additionally gives guidance to frontline employees and others to do whatever it takes to make the customer transaction pleasant and memorable.

Your Service Strategy must have both Core Service and Experience components.

'We make promises and always keep them.' Notice the use of the word 'promises'. It was stated this way to differentiate between what organizations typically say, we give commitments, and what people say, we make promises. It is a declaration that a shift is needed to make the business a people-to-people, or a relationship, business.

The notion of recovery is huge in this strategy. It says that if all else fails 'Recovery will be our #1 priority', and sets in motion the development of a recovery plan that we discussed earlier.

Reflect on each of the strategy statements in this example and see if you can define the behavior in the organization that would have to be seen in order to deliver the strategy. If this strategy were being executed flawlessly, day in and day out, what would you see in the organization? What would people in the service organization be doing? What would the call center employees be doing? What would the technical support analysts be doing?

It is extremely important that once you have your service strategy statements composed, you move to the behavioral translation stage and define, for each department in your organization, the behaviors required to deliver the strategy. This includes the Internal Audit department as well as the customer-facing units. Internal Audit has internal customers, and should be accountable for its part in delivering the service strategy to fellow employees. If your service strategy is not being successfully executed internally, it is highly unlikely that it will be successfully delivered externally, to your real customers.

Create a behavioral translation map from your Service Strategy. Each department in your organization must define the behaviors required to deliver the strategy.

This can and should be an enjoyable process. Educate all employees on what your service strategy looks like when it is alive and well. Hold departmental workshop meetings; present the strategy and then leave your departments to develop the behaviors that are required to support the strategy. Ensure that behaviors are consistent with the strategy intent, and then define how to hold them all accountable. You will find that these workshops will generate energy and team spirit and motivate your employees to actively support the strategy.

Our service strategy was the basis for all communications activities with all employees. We talked to each person in the organization, explained the strategy and why it was so important to us. We engaged our employees in workshops where we broke each strategy statement down into specific behaviors for the numerous service positions we had. This not only drove the strategy home to each person on the service team, but also deepened their understanding of how each one of them individually was expected to contribute to it.

Here is another service strategy example that I helped develop for the North Shore Credit Union, in North Vancouver, B.C.

'We provide quality advice to our members. We will personalize solutions based on unique insights we discover for each

of our members. If we fail to delight our members, recovery
will be our #1 priority.'

This example has many of the features of the BC Telecom strategy:

- Core service is defined as quality advice — advice that conforms
  to what investment expectations each member has.

- There is a strong one-to-one marketing thrust expressed in
  the second statement. The focus is clearly on looking at each
  customer individually, as expressed in the phrase 'each of our
  members'.

---

*If your Service Strategy is not being effectively
executed among employee groups, it won't be
successfully delivered to real customers.*

- Unique insights are the drivers of the solutions provided to each
  member. This refers to leveraging customer secrets. In this case,
  there was sensitivity to the word 'secret' (perceived privacy
  implications), so the credit union chose 'insight'. It works just as
  well.

- The reference to solutions again indicates that this organization
  will be looking beyond just products and services to packaging a
  number of financial services that address a broad set of customer-
  needs plus secrets.

- The credit union intends to personalize its solutions. Again, their
  1 – 1 Marketing theme.

- Perhaps the most interesting aspect of this strategy is in the
  reference to the credit union's intent to develop personalized
  solutions 'based on the unique insights we discover for each of our
  members.' It basically declares that its Be Different strategy is to
  leverage its deep understanding of its customers, and to develop
  personalized solutions for each one, uniquely. Awesome.

Before moving on, be aware that your planned dazzling service
strategy to build customer loyalty can turn into a de-dazzling

catastrophic event in a nanosecond, and leave customers standing with their mouths wide open in disbelief.

Here's my story. I made a long distance call recently using the dial-around service of Yak Communications, an alternative long distance supplier in Canada. I dialed 1010-925, then the area code and the ten digit number of the person I was calling. The point of using Yak is to access lower long distance rates when you expect to be making a long call. Yak very definitely has economical rates.

In this case, I was calling a Shaw call center to question my cable bill. Before my call was connected an announcement came on the line to tell me that Yak had awarded me this call free. Obviously a promotion; I was delighted. This was a bold move on their part to impress me and to convince me to switch to their service.

After this announcement, which I will admit made me feel good about Yak, in my mind a commodity player in long distance, I was connected to the Shaw call center. I waited for a rep to answer, and I waited, and I waited. After five or more minutes, an extremely helpful rep took my call and effectively answered my billing inquiries.

About six or seven minutes into the call, however, our conversation was rudely interrupted by yet another Yak announcement, this one advising me that I had only thirty seconds left on my 'free call'. Panic set in, and my good-feeling bubble burst. I quickly gave the Shaw rep my phone number, realizing that once the call was terminated by Yak, the rep had no way of knowing who I was. Nor did I have any chance of calling back and getting the same rep. Ever happen to you?

The good news was that the Shaw rep did call me back and took care of me. Thanks, Shaw.

For Yak, however, any chance of impressing me enough to switch to them had been annihilated. Yak first delighted me with their free call offer, and then destroyed in a heartbeat all of the experiential equity they had built.

Several things went wrong for Yak. First, I was told that my call was free, not that it was free as long as it was less than six minutes in duration. Second, I was interrupted in the middle of my call to be told that my free period was over. Third, I was warned that Yak would terminate my call in thirty seconds. And, finally, my call was terminated, with the very real likelihood that all the value in my conversation with the Shaw rep would be lost.

I do understand what the marketing guys at Yak were trying to accomplish. They wanted to give the customer a good reason to switch to them, while at the same time containing the financial risks of offering free calls. But they did not consider how their approach would impact the customer. They obviously didn't ask the service people how customers would most likely respond if they were on a call longer than six minutes, like mine. They had no idea what the impact on customer attitude would be if a customer's call were terminated, and the inconvenience that would cause.

Here is how it could have been handled with the customer experience in mind. The initial announcement could have been something like this:

> 'Congratulations, Yak has just awarded you six minutes of free long distance calling. Please enjoy your call on us. After your free period has ended you will be automatically charged Yak's unbeatable regular long distance rates.'

How difficult is that?

The learning point here is to make sure that you look at your promotions and other vehicles intended to dazzle customers through their eyes. Have a customer advocacy panel engaged to give opinions on these types of proposals; it's an investment in time and energy with *huge* payback.

The good news is that there are other companies that get it right; Roche Harbor Marina on San Juan Island in Washington State is a good example. They provide a consistent level of remarkable service every time you enter the marina looking for overnight accommodation for your boat. Deck hands are always there to help you dock your vessel, tie your lines and connect you up to power and water on the dock. Garbage dumpsters are easily accessible and the marina employees are a delight to deal with. The impressive thing is that every visit brings the same level of service. It's all about consistency!

QUICK HITS

- It is critical to define in very precise terms how you intend to serve your customers; what your core service looks like and what service experience elements you intend to treat as priorities. This is the purpose of building your Service Strategy.

- Your service strategy provides direction and focus for everyone in your organization, not just the service folks. Create it, then break it down into expected behaviors in each department and hold everyone accountable.

- Look at the examples provided in this chapter. They are good templates to follow. Constructively emulate them.

- Orchestrate loyalty-building events to ensure that each detail leads to a dazzling, rather than a de-dazzling, experience.

- Invest in Customer Advocacy Panels to scrutinize marketing promotions; look at promotions through the customer's eyes.

Chapter Forty-Three

Now that you have created your service strategy, it is time to begin the journey of execution. In the last chapter we discussed the importance of translating your strategy into specific behaviors to make it more real for each person in your organization. This is a key component of execution, but much more is required.

Execution has more to do with building the right cultural context than with anything else. The nature of your management culture is critical to the success of your service strategy; you need people-intensity to deliver a dazzling service experience. As Peter Drucker observed: 'So much of what we call management consists of making it difficult for people to work.'

How, then, can a traditional company execute its service strategy? It can't. I have always advocated that organizations move from the traditional command-and-control management world to what I call the 'coach and serve' leadership world. In a similar vein, many leadership books espouse the virtues of 'turning the organization upside down,' getting leadership to support employees more and command them less in the day-to-day operations of an organization.

Many organizations draw their organizational charts upside down, thinking that solves the problem. But simply inverting the organization triangle symbolically will do nothing to change the command culture of any organization. Change will only occur if an organization provides detailed direction, most of it which is behavioral, for each manager in the organization. It is this roadmap, rather than the 'brave idea' that will result in positive change.

Organizations must move from command and control management to coach and serve leadership.

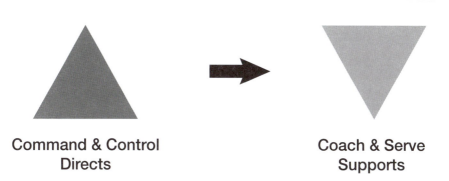

Command & Control
Directs

Coach & Serve
Supports

The command and control philosophy is best demonstrated by looking at the organization chart of most organizations. In the typical pyramid shape, the CEO is at the top and the frontline customer-contact positions are at the bottom. In this model, the company is operated by orders coming from above and being followed by everyone below. The question is, how can you demonstrate flexibility for the customer and empowerment to the employee when they are bound by predefined orders? You can't.

Consider the symbolism of this type of organization. The frontline employees who, day in and day out, control the customer's service experience are at the bottom of the organizational structure, and those who give the orders are at the top. Not a good signal to the organization when you are espousing the importance of serving customers.

The coach and serve philosophy literally turns the traditional pyramid structure upside down, placing the employees who interact with customers at the top of the chart and the rest of the organization below them, in supporting roles. This is the leadership model where management's role in the operational activities of the organization is to support the frontline, either directly or indirectly.

If you're not supporting the frontline, you had better be supporting someone who is. I am not advocating that key responsibilities, such as developing the strategy of the company and other tasks traditionally reserved for the executive, be delegated down the organization, even though I do think that employee input from all levels would provide useful insights in strategy setting. I am suggesting that if it is your objective to effectively execute a strategy that is based on creating dazzling service experiences for your customers, you can't do it from a position of control. You must give control up in favor of coaching and serving your frontline employees, whom you have entrusted with thousands of moments of truth each day.

To flawlessly execute your Service Strategy and dazzle customers, you need to give up management control in favor of serving and coaching your frontline employees.

What does coach and serve really mean? It can be boiled down to the notion that leaders/managers should be looking for ways to make the frontline job easier:

- Empower them to say yes.

- Support dumb rules initiatives.

- Get tough on simplifying customer experience roadmaps.

- Spend time with the frontline, and be recognized by them as someone who cares about them and about their issues. Be their champion.

- Recognize and reward service heroes.

- Develop the training necessary for all frontline people to do their job.

- *Bash barriers* inside your organization; remove the barriers that prevent the frontline from dazzling customers.

- Continually ask the frontline if you are doing a good job at supporting them. Get their feedback on your performance. Have them participate in the '360 degree' feedback process. The 360 program is a formal way of obtaining structured feedback on your personal performance from your boss, your peers, from those who report directly to you and from others in your organization, such as frontline employees, whom you support in some way. The process explores a number of leadership competencies such as teamwork, interpersonal skills, commitment to company values and so on. You would customize the survey to meet your specific needs.

Hold regular *bear-pit sessions* with frontline people, get input from them on the things that prevented them from doing their job well. Then go fix them, and tell your frontline people what you did. I used to dedicate one day a week to be with the frontline, whether it was to meet with a team and listen to their concerns or to sit in with one of them and learn how they did their job. They loved it. We discovered, for example, many dumb rules that were impacting their ability to dazzle customers; these were resolved quickly, and we reported back to the employees who had raised the concerns. I sat with call center operators regularly and listened in on their calls with customers, the nature of the calls they had and how the operator handled them. Amazing people.

If you don't serve the customer directly you better find a way to serve someone who does.

- Hold managers at all levels in the organization accountable for supporting the frontline. Make this part of each manager's performance plan. A significant component of the Marketing Performance Plan and Compensation, for example, should be supporting the sales team. In the same way, departments that provide direct support to call center and service center employees should be held accountable to support them.

257

- Serving customers in a way that builds their loyalty to your organization requires a leadership philosophy of coach and serve rather than command and control.

- The frontline needs you to help them do their tough job of trying to dazzle each customer they contact. You should be asking, 'What can I do to help?' Not saying, 'Do this.'

- Spend copious amounts of time with people in your organization entrusted with managing customer moments of truth (sales, service reps, receptionists, technicians, etc). Recognize them for their efforts and recognize the people who serve them.

- If you don't serve the customer directly you better find a way to serve someone who does.

Chapter Forty-Four

Measure Service Results Constantly

It is absolutely critical that you develop a set of metrics to determine whether you are successfully executing your service strategy. Examine each statement of your strategy and come up with a few key metrics that cover both your core service and the service experience. The behavioral translation, discussed in Chapter Forty-Two, should form the basis for developing your measurement plan. The essential questions you want to ask are:

- For core service, 'Did we satisfy you?'

- For the service experience, 'Did we dazzle you?'

If you don't measure your Service Strategy, how do you know what you're doing?

Most likely you will want a combination of internal statistics and customer perception metrics. Internal statistics can be useful in tracking core service process performance and also as a diagnostic tool for results that you get from customer perception surveys. Customer perception surveys, however, need to be the primary tool to measure both core service delivery and the service experience. Typically, there is some angst about asking customers their opinion on a service factor and then using the result to measure someone's performance and to drive service improvement.

One director of engineering told me that customers' perception of the quality of the voice transmission in a particular region of Vancouver was wrong. He said that the internal technical statistics that measure transmission quality clearly indicate that the quality was 'within limits', and that we should ignore what the customers were saying.

The customer's perception of your service is the only measurement that matters. Use internal statistics to diagnose, not to measure service quality.

The customer's perception of service quality is that customer's reality. Organizations need to understand what drives that response in order to make service improvements. Internal statistics can be useful in this area. They can point you to the reasons why the customer perceives your service a certain way.

Here are some considerations to keep in mind when doing customer-perception service surveys:

- Conduct these on a regular basis, depending on the number of customers that you have. I recommend that they be done monthly for organizations with many customers; less frequently if you have only a handful of customers.

- Include a section in the questionnaire that asks for comments, as opposed to only asking for a numeric rating in some aspect of service. You will get rich information from this extra step, in addition to the quantitative results. For example, I have seen customers recognize employees who went the extra mile for them, provide good suggestions for improving service and point out dumb rules. Customer questionnaires are not always painless to read and accept, but they represent valuable input into your overall service strategy.

   Being recognized by a customer must be seen as the highest tribute an employee can receive. The employee's manager must be made aware of the customer recognition and the event celebrated in the workplace. This will reinforce the importance of delivering to your service strategy, and will provide an incentive for others to emulate the *service hero* being recognized.

- If at all possible, call customers who provide you with helpful insights through their comments. They will be surprised, and feel that you really do care about what they have to say. And you will have an opportunity to discover their secrets.

- The most accurate service perception feedback from the customer comes immediately after they have had the service encounter, when the service experience is still vivid in their mind. If, say, two or three weeks have elapsed since their service experience with you, they will have to recall how they felt at the time, the things that went well and those that didn't. This is difficult for most people to do and will probably distort their perception of your service. The solution is to establish a process that gathers customer perception data at the transaction point.

We used to do this when a business customer called in to have their telephone service repaired. We would send a repairman out to do the required work and, upon completion, would have the customer called right back. The Service Quality Call, as we referred to it, was made to the customer by a dedicated team of people in my organization. The customer was impressed, and we got extremely valuable insights to guide our service improvement activities.

The Service Quality Call gives real-time feedback.

Marriott's Maui Ocean Club in Kaanapali, Hawaii, understands the power of measuring service quality immediately following a customer transaction. In addition to creating a pleasant experience on its website, where you can have an on-line conversation with one of their reps on any subject of interest to you, Marriott presents you with a pop-up survey for you to complete as soon as your chat is over. It is brief, to the point and easy to complete and provides the company with immediate feedback for it to act on if need be.

■ Set specific objectives to support your service strategy and measure the results regularly. Use your behavior translation work.

■ Ask the customer, 'Did we meet your expectations in delivering our core service, and did we dazzle you with your service experience?'

■ Be careful of using internally generated statistics as the measure of your service success. It is no substitute for customer perception data. Use internal metrics to diagnose service problems; use what the customer says as the final word on your service.

Chapter Forty-Five

Measure Serving Customers 'On the Inside'

The road to serving your customers in a superlative fashion, in accordance with your service strategy, requires internal diligence. Applying your service strategy to *the inside* of your organization is a prerequisite to consistently delivering it to the customer on *the outside.* This means serving internal customers the same way as you want them to treat external ones. If, for example, employees are breaking service promises to each other between departments, there is little incentive for them to keep promises made to real customers. The fact is, if you don't do it on the inside, you won't do it on the outside.

Devise and implement an Internal Service Measurement System that you can use between departments that interact in a customer-supplier relationship. I call this 'The Internal Report Card'. I used the concept extensively when I was an operations executive leading operating divisions in BC Telecom.

Consider the following example of how the report card process can be effectively used. The sales organization, in this case the internal customer, depends on marketing, the internal supplier, for a great deal of support:

- An annual marketing plan that provides sales targets by product and service, hopefully moving to Offers. Were the targets negotiated with Sales? Does Sales feel that they are achievable?

- Sales support tools to deliver on Sales targets. This would include things such as access to customer revenue information, propensity-to-buy factors for specific customers, CRM data and so on. Are they helpful? Do Sales find them effective?

If dazzling service doesn't happen on the inside, it won't happen on the outside. Establish an Internal Report Card to measure internal customer-supplier service quality.

- Advertising and customer communications material. Is the overall communications program helping Sales in front of the customer to make a sale? Do the advertising and promotion programs provide a compelling influence to prepare potential customers for the sales contact? Are customers leaning your way after exposure to the communications tactics?

- Sales training. Is it relevant and helpful? Does it enhance the possibility of success in competitive selling situations? Was Sales involved in the development of the program?

- Sales incentives. Are the incentives that Marketing provides to Sales meaningful? Do they motivate Sales behavior and excite them to achieve the results expected of them?

- Availability to Sales. When Sales asks for Marketing help on a particular matter, are they ready and willing to jump in and provide whatever Sales requires? Do they provide quality work?

- Responsiveness to Sales. When Sales calls Marketing to request some information or assistance, how long does it take Marketing to get back to Sales? An hour? A day? A week?

- Customer involvement. Are the Marketing people actively engaged with Sales in visiting customers and supporting Sales in presenting the company's value proposition?

With these interdependencies in mind, you can then proceed to develop an Internal Report Card between Marketing and Sales. Here is what it could look like.

Sales Report Card to Marketing	Rating
1. Value of the Marketing Plan; Sales input in target setting	
2. Quality of sales support tools available	
3. Effectiveness of advertising to support Sales	
4. Value of product and offer brochure ware	
5. Relevance and thoroughness of Sales training	
6. Engagement of Marketing in Sales orientation programs	
7. Value of sales incentives as motivational tools	
8. Speed of Marketing to respond to Sales requests	
9. Availability of Marketing to Sales	
10. Involvement of Marketing with customers to support Sales	

Internal Report Cards build teamwork between key organizational units.

Clearly this approach could be applied to any internal customer-supplier relationship in an organization: HR–Sales; Internal Audit–Finance; Finance–Operations and so on.

In this case, Marketing would develop the report card as it is the supplier of services to Sales. Here's the process:

- Marketing and Sales would discuss the various deliverables that Sales expects Marketing to provide them.

- They would then agree on the priority of each deliverable.

- Marketing would create a report card question for each deliverable. Don't forget the issue of FOCUS. FOCUS. FOCUS. The objective is to land on the few salient deliverables that have maximum impact on Sales executing their job in the field. I used to try to simplify the report card to around six key deliverables for the coming year. They might change for the year after that, depending on the marketing plan and the development of the sales organization. If the report card covers too many deliverables, Marketing will have difficulty focusing their efforts on the key activities required to improve service to Sales: too much to do; where do you start?

- Obtain Sales input and approval for each question to ensure that the deliverable is absolutely clear.

- Decide on a rating system. We used the five point scale: poor, fair, average, good and excellent to rate Marketing's performance on each deliverable question. We used this same scale to measure how well the external customer rated our service to them. It is very important that the internal measurement system mirror the external one; consistency builds understanding and buy-in.

- Include a comments section in the report card. As done with external customers, obtain verbatim responses from, in this case, Sales in terms of how they are being served. As noted earlier, this can be extremely helpful in diagnosing the quantitative ratings and can also serve as an opportunity to recognize and celebrate those Marketing people who are specifically named as providing exemplary service to their Sales brethren.

- Define each rating category. Poor was defined as 'not meeting any aspect of the expected deliverable at all' (unacceptable performance), Good as 'meeting sales expectations' and Excellent as 'exceeding sales expectations' (a super job).

- Meet with Sales to explain the objectives of the report card and the important role Sales plays in the process. Ask them to provide quality and timely responses so that Marketing can learn and improve. The Sales investment in time and energy will pay off.

- Set lofty targets for each question. We used to set 'Percent Good or Excellent' targets with a view to move to 'Percent Excellent' over time. For example, you might have the objective of achieving an '80% Good or Excellent' rating for the sales training that is being provided. Engage Sales in the objective-setting process; they will love to influence how the Marketing folks get paid.

- Present the plan to the Marketing team. The head of the department should do this as a leadership matter to ensure they understand the intent and specific targets of the report card. Have the Sales leader present.

- Send the report card out monthly. Have an independent marketing manager responsible for the process, reporting to the head of the department.

- Present the report card results to the Marketing team, by the head of the Sales department, of course. Compile the results quickly. The presentation should include a discussion of each question: What was the result? What was the target? Why did we either exceed the target or not hit it? What actions should we take to either continue our positive performance or improve our performance to achieve our target? Who should be accountable for the performance improvement activities? When should the key activities be completed?

- Define an action plan to be taken by the department that reflects the results for the month, and follow up on it in the upcoming weeks. Hold someone accountable to do this as a key responsibility.

- Review the action plan each month at your team meeting, when you get next month's numbers. Did you follow through on what you said you were going to do last month? What results did you see from your efforts? What follow-up is required?

If you are an internal supplier of service to another team of employees, here is some advice. Before you proceed down the report card path, have reasonable expectations about the results. Be prepared for disappointing results from your initial report card. This is probably the first time your internal customer was asked to comment on and rate your service performance; they will tend to be brutally honest, particularly if you have not successfully delivered what they have asked of you in the past. Many people avoid the process because of the discomfort and embarrassment in the early stages of implementation.

If you are an internal service supplier, be prepared for dismal results from your first report card. BUT you want your customers to be brutally honest with you.

Look at the results, particularly the early ones, as a level of performance on which you can improve. Don't go into your cave if your early stage result is around 20% Good/Excellent on the sales incentives deliverable. The good news is you have a tremendous opportunity to improve. Figure out what your performance improvement plan looks like, and just do it. As you and your customer gain more experience with the report card, you will discover that your customer begins to manage it as a tool to extract better service from you and to provide you with more constructive feedback; and you will respond by designing more effective ways to serve them better.

QUICK HITS

- If you can't dazzle on the inside of your organization, you can't dazzle real customers on the outside.

- Establish a system of internal report cards between internal customers and suppliers and measure how effective the suppliers deliver their core service — and the service experience their customers have with them.

- Integrate the report cards into the leadership compensation plan, and celebrate the suppliers that do an exceptional job of taking care of their internal customers.

- Don't go to your cave when you get terrible results. Honor the customers who were honest enough to tell you the truth, and set a bold path to improve.

Chapter Forty-Six

Employee Communications: Tell 'Em All about It

'If a tree falls in the forest and no one hears it, does it make a sound?' This well-known expression underscores the importance of communications in the success of a strategy to Be Different in serving customers. It applies, also, to all the functions that we have discussed in the book. But it is of particular importance in the service area because of the number of employees engaged in serving customers and the fundamental and widespread organizational and cultural changes that need to occur to assure service excellence.

If people don't hear about serving customers constantly, they will assume that it's not important and nothing is happening.

The question about the tree falling illustrates the challenge facing you when you execute your new strategy for serving customers. If employees in your organization are unable to see that the projects being worked on are related to your new strategy, they will not be aware of the new path you are on. And if they are not aware, they won't be able to contribute.

What are the communications topics and activities that employees should be made aware of that are evidence that the organization is pursuing a Be Different service vision?

- The service strategy itself.

- Goals of the service strategy.

- Behaviors needed to successfully execute the strategy.

- Successes achieved, and what it took to achieve them.

- Failures experienced, and what has been learned from them.

- Recognition of service heroes in the organization, and what they did to make them heroes.

- Internal report card process, its goals and how it fits into the organization's service strategy model, along with internal service heroes and their accomplishments.

Post customer survey results in the workplace for all to see. Have a conversation about them.

- Results of customer surveys measured against the objectives you have set. Use corporate communications vehicles to talk about service results, and post them in the workplace for all to see. Each department has a slightly different role to play in the various service targets set, so break the overall results down by department so that people can relate to them more meaningfully. If people don't understand how they relate to a result, they are ill equipped to know how to change their performance.

- Executive commentary on the progress being made to Be Different in the service arena. This is the opportunity for the executive to not only support the serve-the-customer vision, but also to become engaged in the process of honoring those employees who play an ongoing and critical role in achieving the progress.

- Stories of remarkable service experiences so that employees get an idea of what dazzling service looks like, and the names of the employees who were involved. An organization that excels in *smelling like customers* in every nook and cranny of their business are obsessive about storytelling. Top management encourages its leaders to get out to the various parts of the organization and tell stories of the truly remarkable service that has been provided. They do it constantly. Storytelling should be an essential piece of a leader's performance plan and there should be training or orientation to show people how to do it. Reward and recognize exceptional storytellers.

An organization that smells like customers in every nook and cranny of their business is obsessive about storytelling.

Throughout this book, I have used stories to emphasize certain points, to paint a picture that hopefully underscores what is necessary for successful implementation of my ideas. In the service area, in particular, stories are probably the most effective and powerful tool to define what dazzling service is and how to deliver it. Certain organizations have made their service stories public in order to communicate to the market their commitment to serving customers.

The Nordstrom example comes to mind. The story that is etched in my mind happened at least twenty years ago. An individual returned a set of winter tires to their local Nordstrom store because they were not satisfied with the purchase. The store graciously and apologetically accepted the tires — even though they don't have winter tires in their product line. They don't sell winter tires. What a memorable story to drive home the message that this company is all about taking care of the customer and solving their problem regardless of what it is. Clearly, in the relationship-building business that means even if it means taking a short term hit.

Another example of a company that is publicizing its service stories — and using the power of the Internet to do so — is FedEx. This is a recent newspaper ad by FedEx used to celebrate their 35th year anniversary:

> OUR TEAM MEMBERS ARE ABSOLUTELY, POSITIVELY THE REASON WE'VE HAD THIRTY-FIVE GREAT YEARS.

'Like FedEx team member Jay McMullin, we strive to go above and beyond in any situation. It's that desire to make every customer experience outstanding that makes our network of companies great. We salute our team for helping us build this network over the past 35 years. To learn more about Jay and other 'absolutely, positively' moments, go to fedexstories.com.'

Brilliant. Stories about people used as a key way to communicate to the world a dedication to create 'absolutely, positively' customer experiences. This is more than testimonial advertising; it focuses attention on the customer and on the employee in a format that everyone can relate to. Go to www.fedexstories.com and browse through the many 'absolutely, positively' stories they have posted there. Amazing stuff.

QUICK HITS

■ Establishing an organization that excels at serving customers requires extremely active and obsessive communications.

■ The airwaves of your organization need to be saturated constantly with 'service stuff': successes, failures and learnings, amazing customers and service heroes.

■ Storytelling is the most effective way of keeping service alive in your organization. Encourage people to tell stories. Provide the tools for them to do it well. Hold storytelling contests. Publish stories for all to see.

■ Hold leaders accountable for storytelling in your organization. Put it on their performance plan.

■ Start every meeting with a story about dazzling service. Get everyone to participate.

■ Have an amazing service story? Share it with me on www. bedifferentorbedead.com

Chapter Forty-Seven

Customerize Your Language

Have you ever listened to the language your organization uses? If you are like most organizations, you have your own dictionary of terms and expressions to describe your activities and what you produce for the customer. Have you ever looked into the eyes of a person who is not a member of your organization and watched them glaze over as you wax eloquently about your business in techno speak?

When I was running an operations division, I had a mission to dumb down the language we used in customer service, specifically to transform the language from internal jargon to language that was consistent with our service strategy. My reasoning was, first, that if we were successful the customer would benefit since we would be speaking in terms they could relate to and, second, we would be introducing another very basic aspect of our service strategy, which was how we talked about the service we provided, which would further reinforce the strategy.

Let me give you a few examples. Define the new term in precise detail so your employees get the picture of the implications of the changed language. This is a great way to reinforce your service strategy and to emphasize the behaviors required to execute it.

- Rather than call them customer complaints, call them *recovery opportunities*. As discussed earlier, a complaint gives an organization the opportunity to respond in a way that builds customer loyalty. Creating new language around the event puts forward the positive view of managing the customer's issue and, as a result, makes more explicit the constructive behaviors expected of people assigned to deal with customers. It is human nature to be more interested in pursuing the positive rather than reacting to the negative; positioning the complaint as a strategic opportunity overcomes the connotation that you are on the receiving end of customer abuse and simply taking the hit.

Have you ever seen a person's eyes glaze over who is outside your organization as you talk about your business in techno speak? Change your language and wash your mouth out with customers.

- Not complaint letters, but *letters that dazzle*. I have always felt that dealing with customer complaint letters was so important in creating or destroying customer loyalty, that I developed a Letters that Dazzle training course that would, first, teach people that recovery was an essential element of our service strategy, and, second, that customer complaints represent opportunities to recover. The course also taught specifically how to write a recovery letter that was directed at building the loyalty of the customer, as opposed to regurgitating company policy.

  It was a straightforward process — essentially a modified version of the service recovery process discussed earlier — which ensured that the appropriate steps were initiated and covered everything from taking responsibility for whatever drove the customer to complain to doing something to surprise them. The majority of the focus, however, was on getting people to understand that responding to a customer complaint is not about quoting company policy. In all probability it was the company policy that angered the customer in the first place, so quoting it back isn't likely to endear them to you. Rather, we emphasized that the letter be written with compassion and understanding and that, if a company policy had to be referred to, the reason for that policy be explained in a sensitive way. This training was an excellent tool in our service strategy toolbox.

- Not calls processed, but *customers served*. Being referred to as a call doesn't exactly convey a customer-driven philosophy. In fact, continuing to use this phrase simply reinforces in employees' minds that this is incoming traffic, typically viewed as a necessary evil as opposed to many individual customers who are looking for help. Change the language, provide the intervention and change the behavior.

Letters that dazzle: a loyalty-building tool to deal with customer complaints.

- Not a repair but a *successful recovery.* Fixing a service mistake or breakdown is simply not good enough. Fix it, and do the unexpected. That's what a successful recovery is.

- Not a service commitment date, but a *service promise.* Remember the first service strategy example we referred to: '...make promises and always keep them'? Incorporating the language change directly into the strategy is a powerful way to underscore the importance of a people-based lexicon.

- Not a commitment given, but a *promise kept.* The issue here is to find ways of underscoring the importance of moving away from a company-to-customer mentality to a person-to-person one. Rather than talk about the company setting the due date for installing a service for a customer, we talked about the people in our organization making promises with other people, our customers. This was consistent with providing dazzling service principles: companies don't dazzle customers, people do.

The above examples were developed in a Telecom-specific context but they relate to any business. Go through your dictionary of terms relating to serving customers. Are the words in your language customer inspired? Do they reflect the intent of your service strategy? How can they be changed to make them more reflective of the customer dimension? Have fun with this. Ask for employee input. Hold a contest to see who can come up with the best customer-centric dictionary. Share your results with me, on www.bedifferentorbedead.com

Companies don't dazzle customers, people do.

QUICK HITS

- Serving customers in a Be Different way requires that you move from a company-to-customer paradigm to a person-to-person one.

- Customer-inspired organizations look for ways to change their language, to make it more expressive of their service strategy. They try to dumb down their vocabulary into words that customers can understand and that resonate with them.

- Start slow, allow the transformation of your language to grow and flourish. Throw the challenge out to your employees. Get their ideas about words or expressions that can be customerized. Hold a contest. Get some excitement going.

- Communicate your progress and recognize the champions who make bold changes to your internal dictionary.

Chapter Forty-Eight

Your Human Resources function, whether fifty people or a single individual, has a critical role to play in terms of enabling the successful implementation of your service strategy. Once the strategy has been developed, HR must examine all of its policies and programs and reinvent them so that they encourage the outcomes expressed in your service vision and goals.

HR must reinvent its policies and programs to encourage the outcomes expressed in your Service Strategy.

I have referred to some of the items below elsewhere in the book, but in this chapter, I want to bring it all together, to focus on each item in some detail. These are specific initiatives that HR professionals can use to produce the kind of motivation required to Be Different in serving customers:

- Leadership development programs should be built on the coach-and-serve philosophy and should transition away from the command-and-control operations model.

- Implement a 360-degree feedback program as a part of your personal leadership development program. This will allow individuals to track their progress toward the coach-and-serve goal. Be Different organizations would include a heavy emphasis on the coach-and-serve dimension of leadership. Organizations use this tool in various ways. Some treat the feedback information as confidential to the recipient, and insist that the individual develop an action plan to improve deficient areas. Others make the feedback information available more widely within the organization, and use it to assess a person's potential for promotion and for any developmental moves contemplated. I think that the power of the 360 tool is in the personal development application.

The 360-degree feedback program is the most effective way to develop a coach-and-serve culture.

I insisted that my direct reports, first of all, participate in the program on a regular basis; that they analyze their results and develop an action plan to strengthen the things they do well and to improve areas requiring attention; and, finally, that they discuss their action plans with me so that I could see that they were getting value out of the program. I did not ask to see the detailed feedback results, but was pleasantly surprised by the many instances when the person wanted to share the results with me, and felt no risk in doing so.

- If your employees are represented by a trade union, evaluate the current working agreement to ensure that it will deliver, through its members your employees, the performance expected of your service strategy. Here are some of the things you need to consider.

  Seniority – A person's tenure in an organization may not determine if they are the best candidate for a service position. Go back to the Vary the Treatment chapter and review some of the people skills needed to deliver dazzling service. You need to hire to this template. If a seniority clause in a collective agreement is a barrier to this, it needs to be renegotiated.

  Overtime – Serving customers is all about the customer, and not about when it is convenient for the organization and its employees to deliver it. If taking care of a customer requires someone to work overtime, do it; if the rules prevent it, fix the working arrangement. I suppose this would constitute a dumb rule as it applies to a Collective Agreement.

Job Prerequisites – Most union agreements define the skills and experience required for non-management positions. A serve-the-customer strategy requires that the prerequisites for all service jobs be reviewed and amended appropriately to ensure your service strategy is achievable. Negotiations with a union to achieve these types of changes can be tough and lengthy, but the results are worth it.

Hiring Practices – Ensure that your job posting process and interviewing methodology are aligned with delivering dazzling service. If the current agreement impedes the ability to fill key service positions fast, and if decision-making tools like interviewing methods require reinvention, get them changed.

Position Descriptions – Are the expectations of the key service jobs in line with your service strategy, or do they require updating and perhaps even reinventing? To the extent that your union agreement requires that any changes require negotiation, treat this as high priority.

- Design the compensation plan with significant weight on serving customers, and that customer perception rather than internal statistics be used as the key measurement tool. As an executive with TELUS, my bonus plan had both corporate and divisional service targets and represented about 15% to 20% of my total bonus package. It definitely got my attention and kept me focused.

- Design recognition programs to call attention to the behaviors and outcomes expected from your service strategy. Include internal service heroes who have gone the extra mile for another employee; make the internal report card process known to all and include it as a formal component of your performance management plan.

- Define your training programs to ensure that the service skills are being taught. And do me a favor: make sure that employee training is never a casualty of budget cuts. All organizations go through periods where expenses need to be reduced in order to meet corporate financial targets, but including training as an expense reduction opportunity tells the organization that training is discretionary, and therefore expendable in the short term, and that you won't see any negative impacts from cutting it. As a minimum keep those programs that are critical to sustain the successful execution of your service strategy.

- In your career development program, stipulate that experience in field operations is a prerequisite for promotion. Those employees who have done their time in the field should be given priority when a promotional opportunity comes along. What a great way to reinforce the 'customer experience is expected around here' message.

- Overhaul your recruitment and retention programs to ensure alignment with your service strategy. Given the intense people component of a successful service culture, who we hire and who we keep is extremely important. Go back and re-read the 'Hire Human Being Lovers' section, under ways to Vary the Treatment, where I covered specific things you can do to hire people who possess the intrinsic skills to take care of customers. HR must play the leading role in reinventing your people acquisition and retention strategies.

- Modify your practices to engage your frontline employees, whenever possible, in the selection of individuals for leadership positions. Their opinions, particularly through the 360-degree feedback process, are valuable indications of whether a candidate has demonstrated the coach-and-serve skills and has a track record of practicing them in the workplace. Furthermore, a frontline employee will definitely know those managers who live for the customer and those that give customers lip service. Just ask them.

- Human Resources — or, if you are a smaller business it probably means you, the owner/manager — plays a critical role in the success or failure of implementing your strategy to serve customers. If you don't have the appropriate people-programs in place to encourage the type of behavior required to deliver satisfactory core service and a dazzling service experience, those behaviors simply will not happen.

- Use the internal report card as a means of determining whether HR is delivering the required capabilities. Measure its performance and hold individuals strictly accountable to defined expectations and performance benchmarks.

- Refer to the initiatives listed in this chapter as the basis for setting your people-program expectations.

Chapter Forty-Nine

BE DiFFERENT Service Roadmap

I've presented a number of ideas to redefine the way an organization serves its customers to achieve a uniquely sustainable competitive position. In order to obviate dysfunction and wasted effort, and because of the multitude of tasks associated with this redefinition, it is critical that all *activities are aligned* both with each other and with your strategic goals. I developed the chart that follows as a useful way to communicate to people what we were trying to achieve through our overall corporate strategy, how the service strategy fits within this strategic context and the essential alignment activities necessary to deliver to our service goals.

STRATEGIC GAME PLAN

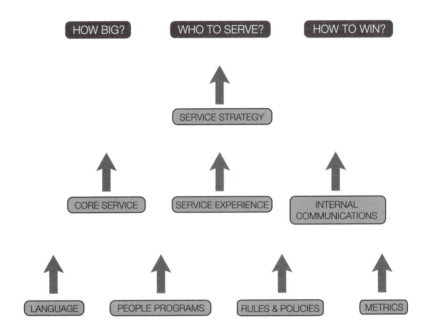

| HOW BIG? | WHO TO SERVE? | HOW TO WIN? |

SERVICE STRATEGY

CORE SERVICE | SERVICE EXPERIENCE | INTERNAL COMMUNICATIONS

LANGUAGE | PEOPLE PROGRAMS | RULES & POLICIES | METRICS

QUICK HITS

■ Someone in your organization needs to own the above chart. This will ensure that there is a robust set of programs in place to serve your service strategy and that everyone is marching to the same tune.

■ How about delegating the task to the service hawk?

■ Establish some high level metrics that will tell you if everything is being executed harmoniously, and that will alert you when things are beginning to go awry.

■ Review performance regularly, and set corrective action plans in motion.

■ Communicate. Communicate. Communicate.

✓ Be Different organizations serve customers, they don't provide customer service.

✓ Look at serving customers as having two components: Core Service and the Service Experience.

✓ Core service relates to the basic thing that the customer gets from your organization, which is generally the underlying capability you offer the market. In Telecom, dial tone was the core service upon which everything else was built. It's a good metaphor for any business: 'What's your dial tone?'

✓ The level of core service provided must satisfy customers, but no more; it is not a contributor to building customer loyalty. Unsatisfactory core service, on the other hand, will send your customers away, abusing you as they go.

✓ The Customer Experience Roadmap method is an effective way to both analyze and reinvent core service. Determine the highest priority processes to work on, as defined by the highest value customers you have chosen to serve.

✓ Consider providing varying levels of core service based on customer value. Your highest value customers should be rewarded with a more personalized service process.

✓ Whereas core service is what customers get from you, the service experience relates to *how they feel* when they get it. This component of the service equation is the key driver of customer loyalty.

✓ The service bottom line is that, in your organization, you need to do both:

- Satisfy the customer with your core service, and

- Dazzle the customer with their service experience with you.

✓ The service experience — simple things that will dazzle:

- Hire human being lovers

- Bend the rules; empower the frontliners to say yes

- Kill dumb rules

- Recover; fix it and do the unexpected.

✓ Create your service strategy to address both core service and service experience elements and to provide focus for your organization.

✓ Delivering dazzling service requires an organization to move from a command-and-control management philosophy to a leadership philosophy based on the principle of *coach and serve.*

✓ To keep your service strategy alive, set bold objectives for service deliverables. Measure your results monthly and, if possible, at the point of the service transaction to get the richest feedback from your customers.

✓ Measure service levels on the inside of your organization. The Internal Report Card is an effective way to dramatically improve internal customer-supplier relationships, and a guide to improving the way 'real' customers are served.

✓ Employee communications is critical to ensure progress in executing your service strategy. Talk openly and constantly about the employees in your organization who are bringing service to life every day.

✓ Create a new language to describe your various service activities. Customerize it and dumb it down.

✓ Human Resources, or the senior people-leader in your organization, is critical to successfully executing your service strategy. Reinvent and align all people programs to it.

✓ The critical people programs that impact how customers are served are:

- 360 degree feedback

- Retention and recruitment

- Compensation

- Reward and recognition programs

- Training

Section Five

BE DiFFERENT Sales

5

Chapter Fifty

It's All about Relationships

Unfortunately, Sales often gets a bad rap in the business world. Rightly or wrongly, the stereotype of a slick, fast-tongued individual who will say anything to promote the sale is out there. And yet the Sales group plays a critical role in the execution of any organization's strategy. We don't often think about positioning our Sales team as a key strategic advantage and often categorize them as 'only sales'. In fact, their role is to get out there and sell stuff. Sales represents a key opportunity for an organization to enhance its business performance. In this section we will discuss some practical and proven ways to leverage your Sales organization to Be Different.

You have two options when considering the role of Sales in your organization: first, you can generate revenue by selling stuff, which I equate to flogging products, or, second, you can generate revenue by building deep and meaningful relationships with your customers, which will result in customers *buying stuff.*

Which behavior has the greater long term benefit to an organization? Which approach will result in more sales and profits in the long term?

We all are familiar with the *product floggers.* They push their products at us without ever taking the time to get to know us, even a little, and what our specific needs are. This type of salesperson clearly wouldn't know a customer secret if it jumped up and hit them on the head. To be fair, the product flogger is the product of the sales culture and overall strategy of the organization; the focus is on achieving product sales and the sales compensation plan is consistent with this approach: Sales gets paid on the basis of how many products they sell.

You can generate revenue by selling stuff or by building deep and meaningful relationships with your customers, who will buy stuff. Which approach creates long term wealth for your business?

Let's look at it from the customer's point of view. How does it feel to be on the receiving end of the flogger's attempt to push a product sale? Do we feel like we want to buy? Do we feel important? Do we feel heard? Absolutely not. We feel manipulated and forced to do something that we don't want to do. Sometimes we actually buy from this person, and hate ourselves afterwards. We feel violated and cheapened.

Do we ever go back to that sales person? I don't. I am not proud of the fact that I succumbed to an intimidating sales approach and actually bought something from this person, but I will never do it again. The flogger won the battle, but I won the war. They got a quick one-time sale from me, but that's it. We're all familiar with musical one-hit wonders? Well this is a *one-sale wonder.* No loyalty is built; no repeat sales are achieved.

Unfortunately, we are not as familiar with *relationship builders.* The relationship builder is a completely different beast. Relationship builders spend the majority of their time getting to know and understand the customer. They want to hear about their issues and challenges. They want to know the customer as an individual. They like discussing the options that are available so that the customer can make an informed decision on the product or service they may be interested in. The relationship builder invests time on the relationship, confident that a sale will probably follow.

From the customer's perspective, being on the receiving end of the relationship builder's energy is an enjoyable experience. You don't feel the pressure to buy; rather you feel that this person is genuinely concerned about you and your needs, and that they are committed to helping you find a solution that meets those needs. In this situation, you actually sell yourself on a product or service, since the result of the relationship building effort is to point you toward buying the product. You are buying; the salesperson is not selling.

It is true that the relationship-building sales cycle is longer than that of the flogger. It is also true that the revenue and profit streams are longer for the builder, since loyalty is enhanced through the trust that is established with the customer. Long term results are more positive; the customer tells others about the experience they have had with the builder, and the viral marketing process begins.

Product floggers push sales at us, but they don't care who we are or how we feel. A one-sale wonder.

There is no question that the relationship-building sales approach is the way to go; it is the way to create a Be Different sales strategy. Focus all efforts on building strong relationships with your chosen customers. Trust that sales will follow from this approach. As a leader, ensure that an appropriate sales compensation plan is developed to encourage this type of sales behavior.

We've all experienced the satisfaction of working with an exceptional salesperson. A few years back, I was in the market for another boat. As my family was growing, I was looking for a slightly larger craft. I enlisted the help of Don Young, the owner of Freedom Marine in Vancouver (www.boatingfreedom.com), to help me locate and choose the best boat for my needs.

Don's company supplied a specific line of boats to the market; he has the distribution rights for the Cruisers line and for a number of other yachts. Given this fact, he might well have exhibited the product flogger behavior. But what happened, in fact, was the opposite. He was a natural relationship builder.

After extensive conversations with my wife and me, Don asked us to document what we would like in a new vessel and what was absolutely critical, the old 'wants vs. needs' trick. He asked us separately about our 'must haves' versus 'like to haves', which provided him with the direction necessary to make his inquiries productive.

You, the customer, actually sell yourself on a product, since the result of the relationship-building efforts point you undeniably at the obvious course of action: you MUST buy.

The amount of attention Don gave my wife was unusual in my experience. Most salespeople in the boat business — automobiles as well — tend to cater to the man. Don correctly understood that my wife played a critical role in the decision-making process. During the needs assessment process, he was a great listener and asked questions of each of us so that he could clarify his understanding of what we wanted versus what we absolutely had to have. Once he had our list, he found vessels that he thought would satisfy our requirements, and he was available and willing to meet with us to discuss each vessel.

He tried to organize the viewings to make it easy for us and our schedule. How refreshing! All the other boat brokers I considered simply wanted to flog their line of boats to me. If they dealt in Bayliners, they insisted on the brilliance of a Bayliner. If they supplied Carvers, they pushed Carvers.

Ultimately, I bought my boat from Don. I was delighted about my decision to purchase a high quality motor vessel, and I thoroughly enjoyed the boat buying experience. I refer everyone interested in buying a boat to Don Young. Viral sales process at work.

The Fairmont Chateau Whistler, in Whistler, B.C., is also into the relationship-building business in a big way and their employees demonstrate it all the time. We are regular customers of the Chateau; the 'welcome home' comfortable experience we enjoy there always culminates with a touch of regret when we leave. We are consistently greeted by name by their employees, who take the time to come by to say hi and ask how things are going. Even when business is hectic, Sarah Wark, Assistant Director of Food and Beverage, and her dedicated sales team always make a point of finding one minute to share with us.

Just like wanting to buy a boat from Don, I always feel it necessary to return the Chateau's caring staff, great smiles, prompt service, amazing food and at-home feeling with buying a meal and recognizing the memorable service we experience there. A large organization that creates Be Different customer intimacy. Very impressive.

Deep intimate relationships = long term profitability.

Here are some simple relationship-building things a salesperson can do to earn a customer's trust and their willingness to enter into a buying mindset:

- Show honest concern for the customer and their issues. There is nothing better in getting a customer to lean your way than showing them that you actually give a damn.

- Get to know them. They are people, not transactions.

- Build a personal profile of the customer. This would include outlining the customer's current situation, with problems and opportunities about their specific requirements defined. It would also include potential solutions for consideration. This does not need to be a complex or arduous task. It can be as simple as Don Young's informal list of our needs and wants for a new boat, or as detailed as a document for a business client outlining the organization's competitive advantages.

- Spend whatever time is required with the customer to get an in-depth understanding of the issues facing them. Don't treat this superficially; go deep to ensure that your understanding is accurate.

- Be an active listener. Ask questions to clarify your understanding of the customer's needs, wants and expectations, and their secrets. Remember, it is critical to go beneath the surface of what customers want, to plunge into the depths of what they desire.

- Take the time to solve problems that the customer has. It is not the most immediately rewarding process for a salesperson to engage in, but customers love it. It always builds relationships and always leads to sales.

How many businesses really get it that the woman is vitally involved in making the final call? Freedom Marine does.

- Be proactive in responding to what your customer wants. This is all about anticipating what is required and acting on it right away. Don't wait for the customer to ask you to do something, get on with it, do it yourself, with a sense of urgency. And make sure that you tell the customer what you did. If you don't, they may never know that you went the extra mile for them.

- Be available to your customer on their terms, not yours. Don Young was there for us at any hour, day or night, to look at potential boats we might buy, regardless of what his own personal time demands were. He gave up a great deal of his personal time to serve us, but it was the investment necessary to get the job done.

- Follow up consistently with your customer. People hate it when they are not kept up to date on matters affecting them. Be a great communicator and advise them of what is going on all the time. This is particularly critical when a problem has occurred and the salesperson needs to act fast and get it resolved. I have known salespeople who quietly and effectively went about turning heaven and earth to get matters back on track, but the customer never knew about the pain they went through doing so. If you must endure pain and agony to make things right for your customer, make sure they know about it. Otherwise, you will never be recognized as a Be Different problem solver.

QUICK HITS

- Relationship building is the only long term sales approach that works; flogging products may get you short term satisfaction, but it will not create a customer for life.

- You have to trust in the relationship-building process. It requires a longer commitment in terms of time and energy, but the return on this investment is huge.

- Strong customer relationships result in customers wanting to buy products from you; you don't have to sell anything except the trusted relationship.

- There are some simple things that you can do to enhance a relationship with a customer. These include: consistent follow-up, being available when the customer wants you, being proactive, problem solving, active listening, devoting as much time to them as they require, developing a personal plan for them, getting to know them as people and showing honest concern for them and for their needs. A lot to manage, but well worth the effort.

- Can you build trusted relationships with customers if your salespeople aren't *people lovers*? Not likely. Find and hire salespeople who exhibit this innate attribute. Apply frontline hiring principles to acquiring Be Different salespeople. If you can't transform members of your existing sales team into builders, by all means replace them with people who are people lovers.

Chapter Fifty-One

Brand Your Warriors

It is interesting that when we think of branding we consider the company brand and branding products and services, but rarely do we consider branding Sales.

Sales represents a critical function in any organization, and should be a major contributor to your Be Different strategy. It follows that Sales should have a unique and distinctive brand that clearly differentiates it from other sales organizations in the marketplace. What is your Sales brand? Branding Sales addresses the question, 'When you think of our sales team, what are they doing that distinguishes them from everyone else?'

Your Sales Brand? What distinguishes them from every other sales team?

Developing your sales brand is a strategic issue. The brand needs to be driven by the Strategic Game Plan of the organization. If, for example, you chose to serve the 'Home entertainment, tech savvy, under-thirty male market in downtown Toronto', your sales brand should address the characteristics of this target market. Presumably you know a great deal about what matters to customers in this segment, including the appropriate sales process that will not only attract new customers but will also increase the loyalty of the existing ones.

Your HOW to WIN strategy should inform your sales brand to ensure that sales differentiation is consistent with the differentiation objectives of the overall organization. For example, if you decided to WIN by being first to market with new technology, your sales brand should address sales attributes such as product knowledge, technological expertise, product migration skills from old technology to new technology, and proactivity, migrating the customer to the new technology early (don't wait for them to ask).

In Sales, most Be Different strategies require strong customer relationship building competencies. Sales cannot support any Strategic Game Plan for their organization without these skills. Here are some sales attributes that could be used to create your Sales brand. Remember to focus on only the few attributes, Roy's Rule of 3, that you think will have a high impact on your customers. Your brand must be clear, concise and easily understood.

- Consultation expertise

- Trusted advice

- Problem solving expertise

- Honest concern for the customer

- Delivery on promises

- Depth of knowledge

- Follow-up

- Sense of urgency

- Being proactive

Construct a brand statement that creates a clear picture of what your sales team looks like when they are performing out there. You need to articulate this concisely and accurately. If you feel bold, you can express this in the *only* statement format discussed in Section One. Don't forget that you need to confirm your claims with your customers to ensure the claims are real, and that you are not fooling yourself. Here are some examples of potential sales brands:

- Our sales team is the *only* one that provides trusted consultation and advice combined with a sense of urgency on any customer matter.

- Our sales team is the *only* one that provides customers the benefits of new technology before they know they need it.

- Our sales team is the *only* one that will lose a sale to do what is right for the customer in the long term.

- Our sales team is the *only* one that fights for the customer inside our organization to resolve their issues fast.

Be bold. Create an only Sales brand.

These are all very powerful brand statements. They define the essential benefits that customers can expect when they do business with you; not many sales organizations act like these.

A sales brand must be broken down into a defined set of sales behaviors. You need to specify in detail the expected behaviors to provide a salesperson the picture of what the brand statement looks like when it is being executed successfully. For example, what is the salesperson doing when they are being proactive, if this is an attribute that you have included in your brand statement? Don't leave it up to individual salespeople to establish their own set of behaviors; each will have their own idea, with the result that there will be inconsistency and dysfunction, as each salesperson interacts with customers.

Formalize the process of defining the specific sales behaviors nece-ssary to deliver your sales brand. Develop a 'Sales Behavior Charter' as the template for all to follow, and be sure to provide as much detail as you can in describing each set of behaviors. Vague descriptions will result in inconsistent behaviors; specific, detailed descriptions will result in consistent sales behavior. It will also provide an excellent platform to develop the sales performance and compensation plan, and act as an incentive to the appropriate behaviors.

If your sales brand was developed on the attributes of consultation and sense of urgency, for example, the following behaviors could be used to guide each salesperson:

Your Sales Behavior Charter: tell 'em how to behave and you live your brand.

Consultation

- Engage in problem solving with the customer.

- Arrange regular customer meetings to define and refine requirements.

- Document what has been agreed to and keep the document current.

- Probe to understand the specifics of the customer's life that may provide insights into the appropriate solutions.

- Get the customer's input in solution development.

Sense of Urgency

- Acknowledge the customer's issue *immediately*, even if you don't have the solution.

- Advise the customer when they can expect to hear back from you.

- Always keep your 'time promises'.

- If you can't, tell the customer you will be late, apologize and get it done.

- Don't put customer matters off.

- In consulting sessions, always skew your action plan to the short term.

In addition, use your brand to define the requisites to look for when you recruit for vacant sales positions. Obviously, you want to hire or promote individuals into your sales organization who reflect your sales brand, in order to get maximum support for your Be Different sales strategy. Use your brand and your Behavior Charter in the interview process. Rank the candidates precisely in terms of how they stack up.

Your brand defines your sales recruitment strategy.

Your sales brand also defines the characteristics of your sales compensation plan. If you don't pay salespeople on the brand behaviors, the behaviors won't be demonstrated and your brand will become wishful thinking.

Your sales brand provides a level of specificity that can be leveraged by your corporate brand. In our above example, the corporate brand can stress certain types of behaviors for which your company stands. Timing of this action, however, is critical. First convince the entire organization that these behaviors should be exhibited by all employees, and then ensure that these behaviors are, in fact, consistently demonstrated throughout the organization. Once you are satisfied that this has been achieved, then move to leveraging these behaviors in your corporate brand.

QUICK HITS

■ Sales are a critical part of an organization's Be Different strategy; you should, therefore, brand your sales team to your target customers.

■ Your overall strategic game plan, Section Two, should inform your sales brand in terms of WHO to SERVE and HOW to WIN.

■ The sales brand defines precisely how your sales function is different from your competitors'.

■ Create a Sales Behavior Charter to translate your brand into behaviors that can be monitored in the field.

■ Use your sales brand as the main part of your sales recruitment process.

■ Back up your brand by a performance and compensation plan. If you don't reward Sales for exhibiting brand behaviors, the brand won't matter and it will not be lived by the sales organization.

Chapter Fifty-Two

Lose the Sale, but Save the Customer

This may seem an unconventional and rarely heard statement, but I believe wholeheartedly that there are times when a salesperson needs to do the right thing and not get the sale.

Ever been in a store looking for a particular product and been frustrated that the vendor didn't have exactly what you wanted? It wasn't the right color. It wasn't in the right price range. It didn't have the precise features you were looking for. You're not alone. It happens thousands of times each day. What do you think the typical sales response is? Check one of the following:

1. 'We don't have one; we're out of stock.' (So leave me alone.)

2. 'We don't carry that model.' (Go somewhere else.)

3. 'We can special order one for you but it will take six weeks.' (Don't take this option as it will be a hassle for me to order it.)

4. 'We don't have the model or color you want, but we have a black one that does most of what you want. Why not take it?' (The product flogger.)

5. 'Sorry, we can't help you at the moment, but I know the XYZ Company in the mall carries what you are looking for. Why don't you try them and let me know how you make out? Actually, I can call them for you, if you like.' (You have died and gone to heaven.)

Unfortunately, responses number one to four are common and don't even come remotely close to meeting the minimum expectations of the customer. They actually destroy relationships.

How many times do you think customers hear response number five? In my opinion, far too rarely, and that's unfortunate because it really does address what needs to be done to build a relationship and dazzle a customer.

Sales indifference is worse than consciously losing a sale.

Be Different Sales Principle #1

Own the customer forever. Taking any action whatsoever that jeopardizes this is simply not an option. We have stressed how important it is to build relationships and that over time these trusted relationships yield very positive financial results. Therefore, it is non-negotiable not to immunize your organization against *customer exit*. Earn customer trust in any way you can.

Be Different Sales Principle #2

Do whatever it takes to protect this position. Even if it means not making a sale. I have seen many occasions where Sales tries to push a particular solution at a customer even though it is not the best fit for the customer's requirements. Trying to force-fit a product or service solution doesn't work, and it eventually backfires on the salesperson because of customer dissatisfaction. The relationship in these cases is impaired because of the reduced trust factor.

Relationship-building behavior would be to bring in another supplier who does have the best fit for the customer's needs. Sure, it might have a short term negative financial impact on you. You will lose a sale. In the long run, however, it is the right thing to do. You stay in control of the customer and you have the opportunity to introduce your solution at some point in the future, when you do have the right solution.

■ Long term relationship building is more important than a short term sale. If you have to lose one, then lose it.

■ Make sure that the customer knows why you did what you did.

■ Plan your re-entry strategy when the time is right.

There are times when a salesperson needs to do the right thing and not get the sale.

Chapter Fifty-Three

Sales as Secret Agents

In the Marketing Section, we spent considerable time talking about the importance of discovering customer secrets; that secrets rather than needs define the Be Different marketing organization. Under customer learning, we discussed the ask-the-customer method of mining each customer contact point in your organization for rich customer secret intelligence.

Who is in an opportune position to gather customer secrets? Sales, in any organization, represents the most strategic capability to unlock secrets, yet they are never held accountable to do so. In a relationship building mode, a salesperson can learn things about a customer that will be invaluable to the sales process, and to their marketing compatriots and service teams, as well. We need to build the secret-gathering expectation into sales responsibilities and accountabilities; sales performance plans need to clearly set out secret-gathering targets, just as you would outline sales revenue goals.

There are a number of specific alignment activities that should be considered to ensure that the entire organization benefits from Sales secret-gathering:

- Sales performance and compensation plans need to be aligned with the secret-gathering responsibilities. This should be mirrored in the performance and compensation plans of other internal

307

departments to ensure that secret information is effectively managed internally and achieves the expected overall strategic benefits for the organization.

- The Sales Behavior Charter should highlight the secret-discovery expectations of the warriors.

- Sales training must cover the strategic context of uncovering customer secrets, and get the Marketing team involved in the training.

- Sales recognition plans should be, in part, oriented to giving tribute to the brilliant ones who made a significant contribution to building the deep understanding of your customers.

- Database marketing capability must be developed to capture customer secrets, to store them and to make them available for others in the organization. Again, in smaller organizations this might involve paper-based repositories and dissemination systems. The form doesn't matter; it's the substance that counts.

Sales must be held accountable for secret gathering; performance expectations need to define secret-gathering targets.

Lastly, your organization needs to have fun with the concept. Create Marketing and Sales *secret agent teams* to gather and utilize secret information. Create competition among these teams, and reward those that do a superlative job. This type of activity goes a long way to building strong teamwork between these two functions, always a challenge in any organization.

QUICK HITS

■ Sales is in a critical position to gather customer secrets.

■ Make them accountable for doing it.

■ Build the expectation into their compensation plan.

■ Ask the customer how well they do it.

■ Feed the information to Marketing.

Chapter Fifty-Four

Get Addicted to Recovery

We dealt in great detail with the concept of Recovery in Section Four, on Serving Customers. The topic requires additional attention here because of its Be Different importance to the sales function.

A reminder: the principle of recovery states that *customer loyalty* to your organization actually *increases* after a service breakdown if — and only if — you do five things:

1. Fix the problem *fast*.

2. Take responsibility for the problem and apologize for it.

3. Atone for your sins by offering a gesture of regret.

4. Resolve the problem to the customer's satisfaction.

5. Surprise the customer by doing the unexpected.

Due to the frontline nature of the function, Sales is critically situated within the organization to take the lead in these recovery actions. They should be known as your *recovery addicts*. When there is a service breakdown, and if the salesperson has established a tight bond with the customer, the salesperson will be the first to hear of the problem and, therefore, the first to initiate the proper recovery actions.

Sales must bash barriers on the inside of the organization to get people to respond to the service breakdown. They must be the customer's champion on the inside to get things done when everyone seems to have other priorities. Sales must also be the agent of *apology* to the customer and must engage the executive, if required, for very sensitive accounts.

Sales should be known as the recovery addicts who are passionate about dazzling a customer after a service breakdown.

Finally, the Sales recovery role must be to identify the secrets that that customer has that will allow the organization to do the unexpected.

This is the piece that blows customers away when there is a problem. The customer expects both an apology and the problem to be fixed, but they normally don't expect an organization to go the extra mile to do something extraordinary. Sales must take leadership by defining secrets the customer has, and then by doing something for the customer that plays to these secrets.

As the executive responsible for the business client organization in BC Telecom, I was involved with the GM of a very large hotel in Vancouver who was extremely upset because our switchboard service had been out of service for a number of hours. When I became aware of the issue, I contacted my sales director to plan our recovery. Once I was satisfied that we had a good plan to get the service up and running, *fast*, I asked the director to tell me what the customer would *not* expect us to do. What would most impress him if we did it?

We learned from the customer's executive assistant that the GM had wanted a special type of telephone instrument for his office for quite some time but, because of other priorities and expense concerns, he had not done anything about it. We learned, also, that the customer was particularly annoyed by the fact that the service outage had resulted in loss of business to his company, even though it was a difficult thing to quantify. His concern in this matter was particularly complicated for me, as utility companies rarely, as a matter of policy, recognize any financial liability in circumstances such as these.

Our recovery plan was to:

- Fix the problem within two hours.

- Present him with a personal letter of apology, signed by the CEO.

- Personally deliver a check for one week of the service that was not working.

- Present him with the special telephone he was interested in, and have it installed during our meeting.

Sales is critical to take the lead in recovery actions.

What were the results of our efforts? The customer was blown away and we had a customer for life.

My final point: given the strategic importance of recovery, why not incorporate it into your sales brand? I believe that this represents a truly Be Different opportunity for the entire organization. Strive for quality (i.e., do it right the first time) and fight to recover (i.e., get it right the second time, *fast*).

QUICK HITS

- Sales should be the recovery addicts for your organization.

- The secrets that Sales discover make successful recoveries possible.

- Make recovery part of your sales brand.

- Recovery must be in the sales performance and compensation plan; otherwise it won't happen.

Chapter Fifty-Five

Say Yes to More Value, No to Lower Prices

Ever heard a salesperson justify losing a sale because the price of the product or service was too high? 'If the marketing guys had only priced this right I would have made the sale.' This behavior is classic in an organization that does not seek to Be Different; price is the factor, in this organization, that determines winning or losing.

Ever heard a salesperson justify losing a sale because the price of the product was too high? 'If the marketing guys had only priced this right I would have made the sale.' It's a sales myth.

As we have discussed repeatedly, *value* is the dimension that separates the Be Different organizations from the commodity players. There are two ways to look at a lost deal; having too high a price is certainly one way. The other way is to consider that the customer is not seeing strong enough value to support the proposed price. As discussed earlier, value is a continuum that describes the relationship between price and some other variable in the organization.

As an example let's look at the Price vs. Offer relationship.

In this case, our price is X but the customer is only prepared to pay Y, which says that they don't see strong enough value in the offer to support the higher price. So, what do we do? Lower the price to Y, or build the offer value to support the price X? Answer? Build value.

The Sales role in the pricing equation is critical. Some may say that price setting is the purview of Marketing, and I would not disagree. However, the setting of value requires active Sales involvement. If Sales suspects that the customer is not seeing the value = price relationship, they have an obligation to find ways to add value to get the deal done. Remember, if the salesperson has done the job as a secret gatherer, they should be able to point the organization in the right direction to add the necessary value to get the job done, be it customized service, additional product features or personalized consulting with a particular problem the customer has. Set up a meeting, *fast*, with Marketing, Customer Service, Finance and Engineering, for example, and determine the art of the possible before the deal goes south.

Never let Sales get away with a suggestion that prices are too high. This is a cop-out from the really tough task of adding value. Sales needs to take leadership with the rest of the organization to provide the value that will seal the deal at the price level proposed. In fact, this obligation needs to be built into the sales compensation plan to hold them accountable to the task.

QUICK HITS

■ Sales must stop whining about losing a sale because of high prices.

■ Sales' role is to show leadership in the organization and add value to support the prices that are being set.

■ Ask the question of your salespeople: 'What are *you* doing to provide additional personal value to your customers to make it easy for them to pay us premium prices in the marketplace?'

■ If no answer is forthcoming, do what you have to do?

■ To all sales people: What is your *value added quotient*? On a scale of 1 to 10, do you add little value to a deal and whine about losing it, or do you add enough value to justify the price set, and celebrate your success when you win it?

Chapter Fifty-Six

Listen, Don't Talk

This is a simple notion, but one that is often ignored by Sales: most salespeople have big egos. We tend to hire individuals into sales positions who are somewhat aggressive, who are confident and who are good communicators. We often spend copious amounts of time with a sales-employee prospect testing them on product presentations and role playing to see how they deal with customer objections.

To Be Different, we need to spend more time holding Sales accountable for listening. How on earth can a salesperson uncover secrets if they are always in the transmit mode — so engrossed and impressed with what they have to say that they cannot hear what the customer is saying as the poor customer tries to get a word in edgewise? There is no question that salespeople need to be good presenters, but they also need to be open to the receive mode, to alter their presentation and discussion flow accordingly.

Do your salespeople attend listening classes? They should.

Does your organization require Sales to attend *listening classes*? It should. Get one of your most loyal customers to come in and lead the classes. There is nothing quite like hearing it from the horse's mouth.

Make sure that listening is integrated into your sales performance and compensation plan. If you don't, listening won't happen, and it will never be developed as a sales core competency.

QUICK HITS

■ How can you hear your customer when you are busy telling them something?

■ Sales ego sometimes gets in the way; the receive mode is more profitable than the transmit mode. So how about stroking egos for listening skills?

■ Sales Listening Classes: a must for all salespeople, and make it a key component of your sales orientation training program.

Chapter Fifty-Seven

Live with the Customer

How can you tell if a salesperson is doing a great job of building a strong and trusted customer relationship? In the business-to-business sales world they have an office in the customer's building. They are viewed by the customer as part of the team, for which office rights are granted. They are judged to be so important to the customer's operations that they must be close at hand so they can participate *fast*, in any issue the customer might have. Salespeople who achieve this status are in a league of their own, and should be held up as an example to the rest of the organization of what sales success looks like. They should be the teachers of relationship building for the rest of Sales and should be a key member of sales recruitment and development.

I had the opportunity to work with a few salespeople who achieved this position with their customers. There was a criterion, however, for making this kind of investment. First, the customer had to express a real need for a Sales physical presence, and, second, the customer had to be profitable enough to us to warrant the investment in the required sales time. Typically, the customers that fit these guidelines were large organizations that had been with us for a number of years.

In the customer's workplace these salespeople were indistinguishable from the company's regular employees, and their day-to-day schedules were driven more by their customer than by me. I involved their customers when performance appraisal time came, and their customers were delighted to participate.

In addition, these salespeople earned a strong reputation with significant currency within our company. They were viewed as customer champions and it was a great deal easier for them to get things done through their internal departments — things such as marketing, service and engineering — than it was for those who had not reached such a lofty position with their customers. These salespeople showed good leadership potential and, as you might expect, were rewarded with management promotions.

Common law relationship between sales and the customer: the ultimate achievement.

In the business-to-consumer world, living with the customer has less of a physical context and more of a real-time communication meaning. Targeted customers experience regular valuable interactions with your organization, getting information on a number of fronts, including new offers available, opportunities to save money, loyalty programs and any other topic guided by what you know about their secrets. As discussed in the Marketing Section, the campaign management process is an excellent way to live with the customer in a virtual sense. Regular, planned and meaningful contact will go a long way toward building strong relationships and loyal customers.

QUICK HITS

■ Whether across town or across the globe, relationships need to be consistently nurtured in order to develop a strong and solid foundation.

■ Find a way to get your salespeople close to their customers constantly, whether in person or virtually.

Chapter Fifty-Eight

Reinvent Sales Compensation or Nothing Happens

Aligning sales performance planning and compensation to relationship-building is so important that I have chosen to summarize the points made earlier in this section. So far, we have discussed a number of Be Different sales concepts:

- Relationship building behaviors

- Branding your sales warriors

- Listening, not talking

- Adding value, not being a 'price junkie'

- Sales recovery

- Mining customer secrets

- Living with the customer

- Focusing on long term customer interests rather than short term sales opportunities

The reality is that if the sales performance and compensation plan does not focus on the customer relationship, relationship-building and the behaviors associated with it will not be a priority with salespeople. If the emphasis is on making the sale then Sales will do whatever it takes to make the sale. I have never seen a group of people in any organization that is more compensation-driven than Sales. This is the way you want it to be. The downside, however, is that if you don't have the compensation plan to encourage the type of behavior necessary to meet strategic goals, dysfunction sets in and expected results are not realized.

The good news is that a salesperson does what they are compensated for; that's the bad news as well, if you don't get the compensation plan right.

One of the most glaring examples of what can go wrong when the sales compensation plan is rewarding the wrong behavior is the financial services market-meltdown that began in the fall of 2008. My observation of this truly cataclysmic and unfortunate event is that financial institutions in the U.S. adopted market share as their key performance metric; this drove all salespeople to flog financial products such as mortgages and other mortgage-derived offerings. Winning was defined by how many customers you could sell mortgages to, rather than in creating shareholder value by developing strong customer relationships and providing good-margin financial solutions.

This incentive plan worked all too well. Mortgage rates were reduced, mortgage qualification requirements were relaxed, people flooded to get into the housing market, market share grew along with un-healthy balance sheets of many financial institutions. *And Sales got bonuses.* They did exactly what they were asked to do — flog financial products to grow market share — and they were rewarded for it. Unfortunately, the market share strategy and sales compensation plan killed several businesses and put the market economy of many countries at risk.

Relationship-building behaviors cannot be punished by the compensation plan; if they are, the aspiration to gain customer trust through relationships will simply not happen.

So, here is a very simplified process for building a relationship-centric Sales performance and compensation plan:

- Develop the sales brand statement, in the *only* format, if you can.

- Define three or four key attributes of your brand (consultation, for example).

- For each brand attribute, define the specific behaviors that represent success (the Behavioral Charter that we discussed earlier).

Be Different Sales: build a relationship-building compensation plan.

- Get agreement to these behaviors, both from Sales and from the executive team. Sales behavior is a fundamental component of the organization's Be Different strategy, so the company executive must be able to understand how the sales force is dealing with customers, and approve it.

- Build the Sales Performance and Compensation Plan based on both the specific sales behaviors that you expect and the outcomes from these behaviors.

- Develop the required sales performance measurement tools. Include individual customer surveys to see if the expected sales behaviors are, in fact, being demonstrated on a daily basis, and if the rate of deep customer relationship-building is aggressive enough to generate the sales funnel necessary to meet the organization's financial objectives.

As the leader of a sales organization, I introduced a customer report card process as a way to quantify sales performance in relationship building. An independent senior manager from my team would meet with the customer and have them complete a report card on the salesperson in question. On the report card, the customer was asked to rate the salesperson on the specific behaviors as well as on the results that we were expecting. This customer rating was then included in the salesperson's overall performance assessment and represented a significant portion of the overall compensation package. Review the earlier example of a marketing-sales Internal Report Card and use it as a template to develop your customer report card. It's easy to do.

The customer should rate the salesperson and determine bonuses.

Your compensation plan should be designed with these factors in mind. But do it carefully. In most cases, this will be a cultural shock for the sales organization; they will be taking a right-angled turn to relationships in every sense and, in most cases, will feel uncomfortable with the behavior-based performance measurement system. A good approach to deal with this anxiety is to engage them in the design of the compensation plan.

A final point. Don't set Sales up for failure by not providing the necessary training and tools needed for success under the new performance terms. If the right support is not provided, desired behaviors and results won't be achieved, and Sales will revert back to the old ways.

SECTION FIVE LEARNING POINTS

✔ It's all about relationships. Generating sales by building deep and meaningful relationships with customers provides greater financial benefits to an organization than sales produced by flogging products.

✔ Brand your warriors. Aggressively leverage your sales function to create competitive advantage. Think of your sales team and ask yourself, 'What are the things they do that distinguish them from everyone else?'

✔ Lose the sale, but save the customer. Do what is right for the customer in the long run, even if it results in losing a potential sale in the short run. The required sales behaviors are to own the customer forever, and to do whatever it takes to get there.

✔ *Mine* customer secrets. Hold your salespeople accountable to discover intimate customer knowledge and to make it available to the rest of the organization so that they can also use it.

✔ Get addicted to recovery. When things go wrong for a customer, Sales gets involved at the very onset of the conflict. Develop salespeople to be the customer's champion on the inside of your organization, to make things right for the customer and to reap the loyalty growth benefits of the recovery process.

✔ Say yes to more value; no to lower prices. Re-vector the sales mentality from reducing prices to get a sale to adding value to get a sale. It's a value game, not a price game.

✔ Listen, don't talk. Salespeople need to be active customer listeners, rather than be impressed with their own ability to give speeches on what your organization has to offer. Remember, it's all about relationships.

- ✓ Earn a spot on the customer's bench. By building deep relationships with your customers, earn the right to sit among them and to be an essential part of their management team.

- ✓ Reinvent sales compensation. Carefully. Salespeople do what their compensation tells them to do. Reinvent sales performance and compensation to explicitly align with the behaviors and outcomes your organization wants to see.

Conclusion

By now, I hope you've written several pages of ideas that you feel will guide you and your organization to Be Different. I hope that you have marked up your copy of this book with comments, exclamation marks and reminders that will propel you on to adopt them in your organization.

The next thing you need to consider is how to move forward and do something with these ideas, as you begin the challenging process of change.

Let the change process begin. A good place to start is with your business strategy.

In a perfect world, I would recommend that you begin with your business strategy. It needs to Be Different to inform the plans and programs for the organization at large and to ensure that resources are orchestrated in the same direction.

I had a client with numerous strategic initiatives the company was in the process of implementing, but it did not have a clear strategy to provide the guidance and direction necessary to ensure the initiatives were relevant, synergistic and going in the same direction. Interviews with many people in this organization pointed to frustration, that too

326

many projects were raining down on them and that they could not understand the relevance and importance of each to the success of the overall business. This dissonance is a concern. How will you know if you're being successful if you don't know where you're going? The figure below illustrates the dysfunction that occurs when initiatives are not synchronized, when they do not all head in the same direction. Lots of activity, but questionable progress.

What can happen   **What should happen**

As an example of the problems that can occur if a solid strategic game plan has not been developed for your organization, consider the implications of not having specific financial goals; of not having agreement on the customer segments you intend to target; and of not deciding how you will compete and win against your competitors. If, for example, the HOW to WIN? question has not been answered, how does the marketing organization develop the key programs necessary to create the desired competitive differentiation in the market? How can the organization's value proposition be established? What do customer communications programs look like? How can a sales compensation plan be put in place? What behaviors does your service strategy stress?

Unfortunately, as was the case with my client, activity was generated through the best intentions of management, and the resultant direction, or mix of directions, filled the void of the absent strategy. If the strategy for your organization is not clear, you can't look up to it and get the project guidance you need to do your job.

However, a perfect world rarely exists in an organization's life. You may not have the ability in your current position to create, or at least revisit, your overall business strategy. You may be in the service organization, for example, and want to establish dumb rules committees to seek out and destroy the rules, policies and procedures that don't make any sense to your customers. Are you stuck? Can you not move forward and implement some Be Different ideas without doing the strategy work for your organization? Yes, you can. It would be highly desirable to go back and do the business strategy work, but it doesn't mean that you can't move forward without it.

If your business strategy is not clear, you can't look up to it and get the project guidance you need to do your job.

If your current business strategy doesn't give you the Be Different direction you need, create some constructive pressure in your organization to review it and test it with Be Different in mind. Or get a group of your colleagues together and try to translate your understanding of your current strategy into the strategic game plan format we discussed in Section Two. Get confirmation that your work is valid, and move on from there. Who knows, senior management might even realize the wisdom of your work and mandate that a strategy review be conducted.

Talk up the Be Different theme in your organization. Generate some interest and passion in the notion, get people engaged. Have fun with this. Marketing people, start working more closely with your colleagues in Sales as you begin your Be Different work together.

Start to customerize today. If you are in the service area, start to discuss the serving customers concept, what it means and the changes you can make to create customer loyalty. Human resources people, or do-it-yourself small businesses, start challenging what the organization is doing. Encourage a Be Different direction with your views on the ideas and approaches you feel will add value to your organization in the long run.

My worst fear is that many of you will acknowledge that there are several ideas here that would add substantial value to your organization but, for any number of reasons, you won't implement them — because they are too challenging, too difficult or may be met with resistance — and will decide to keep things at the status quo.

If you find yourself thinking this way, you are vulnerable to being a change manager as opposed to a *change leader* who takes responsibility for making the changes necessary for a business to survive. It takes guts, energy and tenacity to intervene in the momentum of any business and start the change process. Accept the fact that new ideas are not universally met with enthusiasm and acceptance, and that some colleagues may push back on the need to change. It takes relentless perseverance to implement change. In the long run, however, the results are well worth the effort. The work is essential to thriving and surviving in the marketplace today.

It takes guts, energy and tenacity to intervene in the momentum of any business and start the change process. Accept the fact that new ideas in some quarters of your organization will not be greeted with open arms, and may be received with a sense of apprehension, skepticism and, sometimes, fear.

I mentioned in the Strategy Section that multi-tasking can be deadly; you should pick a few things that you believe will have the most impact on delivering your strategy, and execute them with passion!

There is an exception to the FOCUS. FOCUS. FOCUS. mantra, and this is it: Implementing a Be Different approach in an organization is more about culture than about anything else. It's about raising the energy and passion bar to explore new ideas, albeit ideas with a proven track record of success. It's about making a right-angled turn to customer obsession and it's about creating a *serve your people* ethic among your leadership. In my experience, cultural change requires constant and persistent intervention. It needs different things to be done by many people over a long period of time, and it needs staying the course through strong leadership.

There is no silver bullet in changing the culture of an organization, just as there is no single brilliant idea that will guarantee the survival of an organization in today's world; no single solution or idea that will suddenly, overnight, protect it from demise. Rather, cultural change is a *game of inches*, where the objective is to get as many people in the organization trying as many different approaches as possible, and achieving fast increments of progress along the way.

What happens is that the passionate actions of a few individuals begin to infect the masses; more and more Be Different activity is created and a new momentum begins. This sustainable new momentum, in turn, defines the new culture of the organization: a culture that embraces creativity and innovation, and a business that can look forward to a long and prosperous life.

Implementing a Be Different approach in an organization is more about culture than about anything else.

In my Introduction to this book, I suggested that my work is different from others in the business publishing world. My claim in *BE DiFFERENT or be dead: Your Business Survival Guide* rests on the following proof points:

- My ideas are founded on solid business principles.

- My ideas are proven; they have been successfully implemented in an operating environment.

- My ideas cover all critical functions in any business.

- My ideas are practical; they are supported by step-by-step processes to implement them.

- My ideas are fun; they excite people and motivate them to try them on for size.

- My work is an easy read; the content is presented in my normal, informal communications style.

I've explained how to achieve a sustainable competitive advantage for your organization in order to succeed and, at the same time, avoid premature demise. To both enhance the performance of your organization and to ensure it thrives and survives in the long run, you need to Be Different in the critical strategic aspects of your organization: Business Strategy, Marketing and Sales activities and serving customers.

Cultural change is a game of gaining a multitude of nano-inches of Be Different progress.

One final and important question to consider:

'What is the role of the individual in an organization that is trying to Be Different?'

I firmly believe that Be Different organizations require a nucleus of employees who embrace and live this theme on a personal level. You cannot build and successfully execute a Be Different strategy within your organization if the people in it are living a Be Same ethic, if they are not serving the organization in a Be Different personal way. You can't exercise a Be Same approach to your job and be motivated to take on Be Different ideas and behaviors for your organization.

If *you* are not different, how will *you* thrive and survive in your organization in the face of the massive structural or strategic changes that are bound to occur? The same theme applies equally to *you* as it does to the organization: If you are not different, you are dead (or soon will be).

In my next book, I'll address this crucial component of personal success and fulfillment in the workplace. Be a Different organization, Be a Different individual and employee within that organization, or risk being dead on both counts.

Combine these elements and you've got the roadmap to successfully navigate the rapidly changing landscape of the 21st century business world.

My insights have helped me deal effectively with the constant chaos of organizational change as I've navigated a successful career as a business executive, as a mentor to countless employees and, now, as a consultant and virtual coach to readers like you.

Organizations that survive have a nucleus of employees who embrace and live the Be Different ideas on a personal level.

In the spirit of the *only* statement discussion in Section One, your opinions, responses and experiences are valuable and appreciated and will be considered carefully in subsequent books. Once again, in the spirit of this book, I will personally respond to all feedback received.

Please visit www.bedifferentorbedead.com. Send comments and view further information, including additional services such as a virtual consulting service, seminars, workshops and strategy building sessions by yours truly.

Cheers.

Roy Osing

Appendix One

The BE DiFFERENT Organizational Assessment

The following questionnaire will allow you to see how your organization rates on the Be Different scale. Have some fun with this. Here's how it works:

The key Be Different themes of the book are summarized for you and all you need to do is rate your organization on each. The rating scale looks like this:

The rating scale is 1 to 5 (only integers please; a 3.456 rating will not be allowed) and the definitions of the ratings on the scale are:

5 = the *Be Different* position – you have developed all the Be Different capabilities in your organization. Brilliant!

3 = the *Be Halfway* position – you are well along in your journey to adopt Be Different capabilities, although there are some deficiencies that need to be addressed.

1 = the *Be dead* position – you are nowhere in terms of building the differentiation capabilities we have been discussing in the book. Major action is required to get going.

The intent of this exercise is to obtain an overall impression of what you are doing well in terms of the Be Different themes, and clues as to where attention is needed to get your organization moving in the Be Different direction. Obviously a 4 is a good score; a 2 means you have work to do. You won't find an algorithm that translates your individual ratings into a single score; this would be unnecessarily complicated and would not serve my intended purpose of giving you a diagnostic tool. Rather, each theme is rated separately to retain its individual importance.

I suggest mapping each topic or theme score on the above analogue scale so that you can see if there are any clusters that might imply a certain course of action. For example, if 80% of all of your ratings are below 3, this would suggest to me that you have challenges across your entire organization. If, on the other hand, one-half of the 80% were marketing themes, then follow your nose. Do the cluster analysis and see where it leads you.

Record your scores in the space provided. If you want to have your results charted for you automatically, visit bedifferentorbedead.com and complete the questionnaire online.

Business Strategy

1. You have developed the *Only* Statement for your organization; it clearly defines your unique value proposition for your targeted customers.

2. Your organization competes by offering unique value that attracts premium prices in the market, as opposed to value that attracts lower prices and is provided by many.

3. Your business has decided not to compete on price.

4. Your organization has a Strategic Game Plan that is driven by financial goals and is clear about WHO you intend to SERVE and HOW you intend to WIN.

5. Your strategy has a detailed implementation plan with accountabilities assigned to carry out each activity necessary to deliver the strategy.

6. Your implementation plan portfolio consists of a relatively small number of key projects to achieve your game plan.

7. You have a process in place to regularly review the progress of your strategy and take the required corrective action.

8. You have appointed a Strategy Hawk responsible to ensure people meet their implementation commitments.

9. You have assigned a cut-the-crap executive to eliminate all non-strategic activity.

Marketing

10. Your organization is moving from a pure product focus to a customer focus, where the emphasis is on providing integrated offers of products and services to the customers you have chosen to serve.

11. You segment your market using multiple variables in order to deepen your understanding of each customer in each segment.

12. Your customer learning process uses a mix of the ask the customer and understanding customer behavior methods of achieving a detailed understanding of the customer and what that customer wants.

13. You have institutionalized customer learning in your organization by making it a regular part of your normal business process.

14. Your customer learning process is focused on discovering customer *secrets* in addition to their needs.

15. Your marketing efforts are geared to creating holistic offers based on the needs-plus-secrets of the customer groups you have chosen to serve.

16. You use customer share or share of wallet as the primary indicator of success.

17. You have introduced the customer marketing function in your organization to augment a purely product focus.

18. You have created a Database Marketing capability, and use it to define your Information Technology support requirements.

Serving Customers

19. Your organization has a serve-the-customer orientation rather than a customer service one.

20. You have developed your Service Strategy with the two components of Core Service and the Service Experience.

21. You have reinvented your core service processes from the customer's point of view with input from your frontline employees.

22. You provide differentiated levels of service based on the unique requirements of your high value customers.

23. You have a frontline recruitment process that tests candidates on their innate *love* for humans.

24. You empower your frontline employees to break a rule in favor of serving a customer, and your organization rewards them for doing so.

25. You have taken action on the dumb rules in your organization that upset your customers; a senior leader is the champion of the cause.

26. You have a *coach and serve* rather than a command and control leadership philosophy.

27. Serving customer objectives are established and results are measured regularly.

28. You use some type of internal report card to measure how well internal customers are served.

29. Objectives for serving customers are included in all leadership compensation plans and carry a significant weight.

30. The people programs in your organization have been developed to encourage the behaviors required by your service strategy.

31. Your organization has customerized its language to rid it of internal techno speak and make it more customer-inspired.

Sales

32. Your sales function is focused on developing customer *relationships* as opposed to flogging products.

33. You have created your Sales brand and it is an integral part of your go-to-market strategy.

34. Your organization's Sales performance plans target relationship-building outcomes.

35. Sales compensation in your business is driven by relationship-building behaviors.

36. Customer perception feedback is the main measure of how well Sales demonstrates relationship-building behaviors.

37. Sales and Marketing use an internal report card to measure the quality of service they provide to one another.

38. Sales is held accountable for secret gathering and is recognized by their Marketing colleagues for their efforts.

39. Sales has explicit recovery accountabilities in their performance plans.

40. Sales uses some type of customer report card to gather customer feedback on Sales' performance.

Appendix Two

BE DiFFERENT Organizations Cited

Index

+3403

www.bedifferentorbedead.com

About the Author

A leading executive in the Canadian telecommunications industry and a recognized business consultant and educator, Roy Osing's career spans over three decades of singular achievement.

During his distinguished tenure with TELUS, Osing served as chief marketing officer, senior vice president for Strategic Alliance Management, and executive vice president and president of TELUS Advanced Communications. Osing developed multiple strategic partnerships and alliances with major corporations over the years, and was responsible for exponential growth in emerging data and internet businesses, successfully positioning TELUS as a global leader in the industry.

Osing was senior vice president marketing of the former BC Telecom. Under his leadership, the company received the 1998 American Marketing Association's "Marketer of the Year Award" in British Columbia.

A graduate of the University of British Columbia with degrees in mathematics and computer science, Osing is founding chair and president of the British Columbia Quality Council. He is a former member of the board of directors of the Vancouver Board of Trade, the British Columbia Technology Industry Association, the British Columbia Cancer Foundation, and the British Columbia & Yukon Heart and Stroke Foundation.

Roy Osing is founder, president and chief executive officer of Brilliance for Business, an organization dedicated to providing practical and proven ways to improve both business and personal performance.